W9-BLG-125

The Jossey-Bass Nonprofit and Public Management Series also includes:

Transforming Fundraising: A Practical Guide to Evaluating and Strengthening Fundraising to Grow with Change, Judith E. Nichols

How to Write Successful Fundraising Letters, Mal Warwick

The Five Strategies for Fundraising Success, Mal Warwick

Creating Your Employee Handbook, The Management Center, Leyna Bernstein

The Drucker Foundation Self-Assessment Tool for Nonprofit Organizations, Revised Edition, The Peter F. Drucker Foundation for Nonprofit Management

Boards That Make a Difference: A New Design for Leadership in Nonprofit and Public Organizations, Second Edition, John Carver

Winning Grants Step By Step, Mim Carlson

Forging Nonprofit Alliances, Jane Arsenault

Conducting a Successful Capital Campaign, Second Edition, Kent E. Dove

Fund Raisers: Their Careers, Stories, Concerns, and Accomplishments, Margaret A. Duronio, Eugene R. Tempel

Creating Caring and Capable Boards, Katherine Tyler Scott

The Fundraising Planner: A Working Model for Raising the Dollars You Need, Terry and Doug Schaff

The Insider's Guide to Grantmaking, Joel J. Orosz

The Jossey-Bass Handbook of Nonprofit Leadership and Management, Robert D. Herman and Associates

The Jossey-Bass Guide to Strategic Communications for Nonprofits, Kathleen Bonk, Henry Griggs, Emily Tynes

Marketing Nonprofit Programs and Services, Douglas B. Herron

The Budget-Building Book for Nonprofits, Murray Dropkin, Bill La Touche

Strategic Planning for Public and Nonprofit Organizations, John M. Bryson

Achieving Excellence in Fund Raising, Henry A. Rosso and Associates

The Grantwriter's Start-Up Kit, Creed C. Black, Tom Ezell, Rhonda Ritchie

Secrets of Successful Grantsmanship, Susan L. Golden

Demystifying Grant Seeking

Demystifying Grant Seeking

WHAT YOU **REALLY** NEED TO DO
TO GET GRANTS

Larissa Golden Brown
Martin John Brown

Foreword by Judith E. Nichols, Ph.D., CFRE

JOSSEY-BASS
A Wiley Company
San Francisco

Published by

JOSSEY-BASS
A Wiley Company
989 Market Street
San Francisco, CA 94103-1741

www.josseybass.com

Jossey-Bass books and products are available through most bookstores. To contact Jossey-Bass directly, call (888) 378-2537, fax to (800) 605-2665, or visit our website at www.josseybass.com.

Substantial discounts on bulk quantities of Jossey-Bass books are available to corporations, professional associations, and other organizations. For details and discount information, contact the special sales department at Jossey-Bass.

We at Jossey-Bass strive to use the most environmentally sensitive paper stocks available to us. Our publications are printed on acid-free recycled stock whenever possible, and our paper always meets or exceeds minimum GPO and EPA requirements.

The excerpt describing the history of The Orlo Foundation in Chapter Four is used with permission by The Orlo Foundation.

Exhibit 5.1 in Chapter Five is reprinted with permission from Dragon's Breath International.

Library of Congress Cataloging-in-Publication Data
Brown, Larissa Golden, date-
   Demystifying grant seeking: what you really need to do to get grants /
Larissa Golden Brown, Martin John Brown.—1st ed.
       p. cm.—(Jossey-Bass nonprofit and public management series)
Includes bibliographical references and index.
   ISBN 0–7879–5650–3 (alk. paper)
   1. Fund raising.   2. Proposal writing for grants.   I. Brown, Martin
John, date-   II. Title.   III. Series.
   HG177 .B767 2001
       658.15'224—dc21   2001002015

FIRST EDITION
HB Printing   10 9 8 7 6 5 4 3 2 1

The Jossey-Bass
Nonprofit and Public Management Series

CONTENTS

Figures and Exhibits   xi

Foreword   xiii
  Judith E. Nichols, Ph.D., CFRE

About the Authors   xv

Acknowledgments   xvii

Introduction: Who This Book Is For and How to Use It   xix

PROLOGUE Get Inspired and Ready to Go   1

  1. Clear Away Myths and Fears   3

  2. Understand the Grant-Seeking Cycle   17

  3. Set Up a Simple Office   23

STEP ONE Learn About Your Organization, Community,
  and Funders   33

  4. Learn About Your Organization and Programs   35

  5. Synthesize What You've Learned So Far   59

  6. Learn About Your Community   69

  7. Learn About Funders   77

STEP TWO Match Your Request to a Funder   95

  8. Move from Lead to Prospect to Match   97

STEP THREE Invite a Funder to Invest in Your Organization   109

  9. Invite a Funder to Give   111

10. Guide Relationships, Meetings, and Tours   135

STEP FOUR Follow Up with Your Organization and Your Funder   145

11. Communicate After Mailing a Proposal   147

12. Follow Up After a Funding Decision   155

STEP FIVE Evaluate Your Results, Methods, and Opportunities   163

13. Evaluate the Past, Strategize the Future   165

14. Personalize Your Grant-Seeking Cycle   173

15. Set Your Grant-Seeking Ground Rules   179

EPILOGUE Get Inspired All Over Again   193

16. Grow from Efficiency to Expertise   195

Notes   201

Resource A: Hands-On Forms for Grant Seekers   205

Resource B: Complete Sample Grant Proposal   221

Index   237

FIGURES AND EXHIBITS

FIGURES

2.1	The Grant-Seeking Cycle	18
3.1	A Simple Grant-Seeking Office	25

EXHIBITS

5.1	Organizational Resume	64
5.2	Program Resume	66
9.1	Sample Project Budget	122
10.1	Project Summary Form	141
11.1	Overall Tracking Form	149
12.1	Grant Follow-Up Form	159
A.1	Questions About Our Organization	206
A.2	Questions About Our Program	208
A.3	Considering a Match	210
A.4	Proposal Assembly Form	212
A.5	Fifteen Steps to a Proposal Narrative	213
A.6	Project Summary Form	214
A.7	Overall Tracking Form	215
A.8	Grant Follow-Up Form	216
A.9	Staff Reminder Form	217
A.10	Grant-Seeking Ground Rules	218

To our parents,
David and Eileen Golden,
and
Daniel and Arvilla Brown

FOREWORD

Grant seeking relies more on knowing what to *do* than how to *write.* Yet most fundraisers don't understand the importance of organizing their grant-seeking efforts. By focusing on writing and putting their energy into a few long-shot grant proposals that are eloquently written but poorly targeted or timed, they waste energy and set themselves up for disappointment. I've seen this happen again and again in nonprofits of all sizes, which is why I'm pleased to welcome *Demystifying Grant Seeking* into the library of books available on grants.

This book makes a special contribution to an often misunderstood field. Larissa and Martin Brown focus on the logical aspects of grant seeking, that is, how to control the flow of information to bring together the best of office organization techniques and development expertise. They help people with all levels of experience set aside the fear and time-stealing habits that keep them from raising serious money.

And the authors do it with integrity. Their book sets aside the myth that grants result from adulating foundation trustees, playing games of chance, and designing programs that meet funders' desires. It frees the reader from the fear of having to know the right people or the right jargon. The book suggests that fundraisers should rely on something much easier to come by: their own common sense and heart.

The book suggests approaching grant seeking with honesty, logic, and passion.

I first met Larissa Brown in 1998, when she came to work for me at The Salvation Army, Cascade Division. I told her we needed to transform our grants effort, and I gave her a goal to take our modest $300,000-a-year grants program to over $1 million in just twelve months. When that year was through, we had reached $1.7 million in cash gifts and had received a $1.25-million in-kind gift.

Some people can see the big picture and some see details, but Larissa has that rare ability to see both and to move between them. It took both dreaming and planning to break our $1-million goal. This combination of talents comes through in Larissa's contribution to *Demystifying Grant Seeking,* where she gives the reader inspiration to embrace the larger purpose of grants, as well as step-by-step instructions for approaching the task.

Martin's background is in science and journalism. His ability to explain complex procedures in a clear way and his remarkable ability to engage readers in subjects that are hard to understand make *Demystifying Grant Seeking* a pleasure to read. Unlike many instructional books, this one actually makes the reader eager to put pen to paper. Coming from outside the fundraising arena, Martin contributes an objective viewpoint to the subject of grant seeking, which is too often burdened with assumptions lacking foundation.

I believe *Demystifying Grant Seeking* will be of interest to a broad group of fundraisers, including those new to grant seeking and those who have been successful in past grant efforts but need to reinvigorate their practice. Those who already own a number of books on grant writing will find this one to be a refreshing complement. Anyone who needs a fresh start, an infusion of hope and energy, and a clear step-by-step plan will be pleased to have found *Demystifying Grant Seeking.* It is a rare book that offers all these elements.

Portland, Oregon   Judith E. Nichols, Ph.D., CFRE
July 2001

ABOUT THE AUTHORS

LARISSA GOLDEN BROWN helps nonprofit organizations in the Pacific Northwest streamline their grant seeking. She has written grant proposals and case statements for six years and in that time has helped people raise more than $5 million to fund their missions and dreams. Her employers and clients have included the Oregon Children's Foundation, The Salvation Army, Community Outreach, Inc., and Sisters of the Road Cafe. Working with the Portland consulting firm C3 Strategies, Larissa has written case statements for major campaigns by clients, including the City Club of Portland, Portland Opera, Talking Book and Braille Services of the Oregon State Library, the Intertribal Timber Council, and Portland Waldorf School.

Larissa is a graduate of Drew University in New Jersey. She is a board member of the Willamette Valley Development Officers—a professional resource organization with more than 580 members—and a charter member of the American Association of Grant Professionals. She also volunteers as a board member with The Orlo Foundation, a grassroots nonprofit that uses the creative arts to explore environmental issues. When not working on grants, she makes mixed-media sculptures, studies demography at Portland State University, and paddles on an international dragon boat racing team with her husband and coauthor, Martin.

MARTIN JOHN BROWN is a scientist turned writer with a background in forest ecology and a degree from McGill University. His original research has appeared in *American Naturalist* and the *Journal of Ecology*. Brown is an ecological consultant whose clients have included the Smithsonian Environmental Research Center and the Pacific Northwest Research Station of the U.S. Forest Service. He also served as a crisis line and homeless shelter supervisor for Community Outreach, Inc.

In recent years he has moved into environmental journalism and creative writing. His work has appeared in *High Country News, Venue,* and other publications; he serves as an editor for Portland's acclaimed journal of arts and environment, *The Bear Deluxe.* Brown's fiction has been rewarded with fellowships at the Millay Colony and the New York Mills Regional Cultural Center.

ACKNOWLEDGMENTS

This book would not exist without the guidance and friendship of Betsy and George Wright of the Portland consulting firm C3 Strategies. They gave me (Larissa) my first consulting jobs and have encouraged and assisted Martin and me through the writing and publishing of *Demystifying Grant Seeking*.

Martin and I developed the principles and practices in this book with the cooperation of nonprofit leaders who believed in us and let us practice and test our grant-seeking system on their programs. We are especially grateful to Patty K. Pate and Doni Reisland of Community Outreach, Inc., and Genny Nelson and Christine Fry of Sisters of the Road Cafe.

We also extend our thanks to Charline McDonald of Meyer Memorial Trust, who first requested that I create a one-page summary of my entire organization—an activity that now forms an important part of this book. Victor Merced and Alice McCartor of Meyer Memorial Trust and Kathleen Cornett of the Oregon Community Foundation have also been influential in the development of the habits that make up the backbone of the book.

Another nonprofit leader who helped give a real test to the principles in this book is Judith E. Nichols. Her faith and encouragement, along with that of our friends and colleagues Jeanmarie and Stan Williams, Jacinta Chvatal, Melissa Rose, Ellen Bussing, Tom Webb, Amy Brown, and Jamaal T. Folsom, made the completion of this book possible. It's been a great experience working with and enjoying the support of all these remarkable people.

Finally, we'd like to thank our friends, particularly those at Orlo and those on our dragon boat team, who have put up with our absence while we finished this book. We'll see you on the water!

Portland, Oregon   Larissa Golden Brown
July 2001   Martin John Brown

INTRODUCTION: WHO THIS BOOK IS FOR AND HOW TO USE IT

This is not your average book about grants. Most books about grants concentrate on the art of writing proposals, and a few present grants from the point of view of the foundations that make them. Although this book touches on those subjects, it concentrates on something that is at least as important when it comes to raising money but is rarely discussed in print: the principles behind successful grant seeking. We describe a system, based on those principles, that makes year-round grant seeking productive and agony-free. This book walks you through setting up this system in your office and explores the reasons why it works.

The book is titled *Demystifying Grant Seeking* because it's all about setting aside the paralyzing myths and mysteries that surround grants and getting down to the work at hand. You will demystify grants by *doing*—by organizing your office and practicing the right work habits so you can get more and better grant proposals out the door and more money coming in, without suffering. By the time you've finished working through the book's exercises, you will know from experience how to seek grants with efficiency and integrity, and you will own a working system that supports and reflects your new perspective.

This is a book for starting or revamping a grant-seeking effort. It's for you if you're a nonprofit fundraiser or executive who's mystified or agonized by grants or the effort it takes to win them, or if you feel unafraid but your grants effort has somehow gotten stalled. Because it teaches you how to divide your time among tasks, this book may be especially useful if you are a staff person (at any level, from CEO to intern) who is expected to dedicate *some* of your time to grants, or if you are a volunteer who has agreed to take on grant seeking for an organization you believe in. Although this book was written with small- to medium-sized human service and arts-related nonprofits in mind, the principles explored are applicable to nonprofits of any size and orientation.

THE BOOK'S SECTIONS AND CHAPTERS

This book's sections and chapters are organized around the five basic steps in the cycle of systematic grant seeking. But before you can begin working in that cycle, you need to prepare on both mental and practical levels. The first section of the book— "Get Inspired and Ready to Go"—helps you do that.

In Chapter One we introduce you to the world of grant seeking by dismissing common myths and fears about it. You learn what you should expect from the process and some constructive ways to approach it. We argue that in contrast to all the hype, grants are fair deals between colleagues with similar interests, and the steadiness and integrity of your efforts will be rewarded.

Chapter Two provides a context for your grant seeking by describing a five-step grant-seeking cycle you will go through again and again. In plain language it gives you the framework for the system you will set up in the next several chapters.

Chapter Three describes a more physical kind of preparation. Here you begin to extend ideas into action by rolling up your sleeves and setting up your office space. We specify all the necessary materials, right down to the file folders you need to make. The detail is important because each part of your office will physically reflect an element of effective grant seeking. You don't need any specialized databases or fundraising software; you just need everyday office supplies and a computer.

Now you're ready to go through the steps of the grant-seeking cycle for the first time. In the section "Step One: Learn About Your Organization, Community, and

Funders," you begin handling the information that is the basis of all good grant proposals. In particular you gather information about your organization's needs and strengths, your community and its needs, and your potential funders and their goals. Any grant proposal must demonstrate a basic compatibility among those three areas.

Chapter Four is where you learn about your organization and its programs; you begin asking targeted questions of your CEO and program staff and choosing one top-priority program to be your initial focus for grant seeking.

In Chapter Five you practice your grant-writing skills in a low-pressure environment, synthesizing information about your organization and first-priority program into short "resumes," biographies, and other items. These become the foolproof base materials you will use to build all your future grant proposals.

Chapter Six leads you through learning about the community conditions your organization addresses, whether your community is as small as a one-stoplight town or as big as all humanity. When you know the authentic needs of your community, you know what makes your organization's work meaningful and important; you will then find it easier to write compelling proposals.

In Chapter Seven you learn to research the funders that can help your organization and community address their needs. As you generate your first ten funding leads, you also learn to control the information that's flowing into your office so it doesn't overwhelm you.

Once you've established a basic compatibility between community, organization, and a potential funder, your next step is to zero in on the specific items that a funder will find compelling. "Step Two: Match Your Request to a Funder" is described in Chapter Eight. Here you put all your recent research to work. Out of your organization's many needs, you determine which ones the funder will find exciting and natural to fund. Now you know exactly what your grant proposal will ask the funder to pay for.

The next step is making your formal request for a grant. In "Step Three: Invite a Funder to Invest in Your Organization," you learn the various forms this request can take. Writing a full grant proposal is usually necessary, but your invitation to the funder could also include phone calls, a letter of inquiry, or face-to-face meetings.

Chapter Nine covers your initial contacts and written communications with a funder. The chapter takes you through the proposal assembly and writing process, which, given all your preparation, may be a lot easier than you once imagined.

Chapter Ten discusses more personal parts of your invitation to the funder. You learn how to look for and manage the kind of relationships that could help or hurt your proposal's chances and to manage in-person meetings and site visits.

Making the invitation is not the end of your grant-seeking process. Follow-up is essential. In "Step Four: Follow Up with Your Organization and Your Funder" you learn how to manage post-proposal communications. In Chapter Eleven you find out how to track the status of your grant requests and communicate with your colleagues about them. Within your organization you need to keep people informed about the process and involved in it.

In Chapter Twelve you practice what to do once you receive a response from a funder, whether it's in the form of a check in the mail, an invitation to submit a full proposal, a request for a visit to see your program in action, or a flat-out rejection. In all cases you want to keep the funder engaged in your organization's work and cultivate a collegial relationship.

Before you go back to the beginning of the grant-seeking cycle to pursue another grant opportunity, it's important to pause to see what you can learn. In "Step Five: Evaluate Your Results, Methods, and Opportunities" you analyze your experience to find how your future work can be improved. Why did you (or didn't you) get the grant? It is often possible to find out. How can you improve your work? What are your next opportunities, and how should you pursue them?

Chapter Thirteen addresses how to appraise your next opportunities and upcoming deadlines. You choose the next grant request you'll focus on. You also learn how to evaluate your work as a grant seeker and set meaningful financial and nonfinancial grant goals.

Chapter Fourteen encourages you to reap the rewards of all your recent experience. Now that you understand the grant-seeking cycle, you can put together a guide for your next year of grant-seeking work—a calendar of daily, weekly, and monthly activities that will result in fewer surprises, more completed grant proposals, and more sleep.

As your grant-seeking office gets more productive, you'll discover a need to work out some organizational policies for your collaborations with other people at your organization, from major tasks like designing programs and setting fundraising priorities to details like signing proposals. Chapter Fifteen shepherds you through the process of creating those policies so that everyone knows exactly when and how they will be expected to participate.

Your effectiveness and efficiency as a grant seeker won't be the result of some secret knowledge or magic but will flow from simple and powerful habits like respecting time and clearing away the fuss and extra work from your grants system. Chapter Sixteen, which constitutes the short section "Get Inspired All Over Again," gathers the habits that have been introduced gradually throughout the book and discusses them in a single essay. The chapter encourages you to take your grant seeking beyond the merely efficient and effective into the truly artful.

Finally, reproducible versions of the worksheets and forms you have used throughout the book appear in Resource A, and a complete sample grant proposal appears in Resource B. You can see that a persuasive proposal is more than just a well-written narrative.

DEFINITIONS AND ASSUMPTIONS

So that we can explain things concisely, we make some assumptions in this book about who you are, the kind of place you work, and the kind of grants you're seeking.

First, we assume you work or volunteer for a *charitable nonprofit organization,* where you are partly or wholly responsible for seeking grants, and that you have some time each week to work on that task. You work for or with your organization's *chief executive officer* (CEO), who is often called the *executive director.* The CEO works with and is responsible to your organization's *board of directors* (*board* for short). Your organization works toward the general benefit of one or more *communities,* which can be defined geographically or in other terms. Examples are "the people of Oregon" and "struggling artists everywhere."

The grant funds you are seeking usually come from *charitable foundations*— either independent, private foundations (with endowments derived from a single source, such as a family) or *community foundations* (publicly sponsored, with contributions received from many donors).[1] Your grant funds may also come from *corporations* or *corporate foundations* (independent grant-making organizations with close ties to the corporation providing funds).[2] We call these sources *grant makers* or *funders.* Although the principles of the book can be applied to government grant seeking, that is not our focus. It is useful to note that not all organizations with the word *foundation* in their names are grant makers; many are operating foundations—organizations much like yours that implement their own programs. (For a table that clearly compares the various types of foundations, see the introductory pages of the *Foundation Directory*, published by The Foundation Center.)

Your organization probably has several different *programs* or *projects*. For example, if your organization is devoted to local hiking trails, it might have one program that publishes guidebooks to the trails and another that coordinates volunteers to maintain the trails. This book uses the words *program* and *project* interchangeably.

These programs and projects will be the basis of most of your grant requests, and they may be of several kinds. You may have *mission-based programs* in which you provide some kind of experience or service to people, groups, the public, community, or world. We define this category very broadly to include everything that is an actual service or activity that fulfills your mission, from arts performances and exhibits to soup kitchens, from home fix-it fairs to rose test gardens. This will include ongoing programs and one-time special projects.

In addition to your mission-based programs, you may have *capital projects* that involve purchasing or upgrading physical items with long-term monetary value, such as computers or industrial dishwashers, or you may have what we refer to as *major capital campaigns* to raise funds for entire buildings, sites, groups of buildings, or renovations.

Finally, you may have *internal projects* that are important to the operation of your mission-based programs but that do not serve or involve a constituency or public in direct pursuit of your mission. These might include staff training, purchasing mailing lists, or creating a development department and broadening your funding base. The latter are sometimes called *technical assistance* projects if they involve enhancing specific skills or meeting networking needs (for example, with workshops, conferences, or new business cards). They may be called *capacity-building* projects if they involve increasing your organization's capacity to carry out its mission (for example, with fundraising staff or board development).

This book focuses on grants for mission-based programs and smaller capital projects, which are convenient and appropriate places for you to learn the basics of systematic grant seeking. These are the kinds of grants most frequently made by the abundance of small and local foundations available in your area. If you are raising funds for a major capital campaign or an internal project, this book may not have all the detailed information you need, but its principles and practices still apply.

This book makes a distinction between the kinds of staff at your organization. *Program staff* have the primary responsibility of planning and running the programs that fulfill your organization's mission, and *development staff* have the primary responsibility of raising the money and other resources to pay for your organization and support its programs. (We call them development staff rather than fundraising staff to emphasize their role in developing long-term resources, not just quick cash.) If your organization is small enough that the program staff and development staff are mostly the same people (maybe even just you), you can still use this book, *as long as you remember the difference between your roles.*

It's useful to remember that grant makers, particularly foundations of significant size, involve many people and many different roles. The *trustees* of a foundation are generally its board of directors; they are ultimately responsible for the way the foundation gives out money. However, they may be assisted in reviewing and judging requests for money by staff, whom we call *foundation staff* or *program officers*. In a few cases trustees may delegate funding decisions to these staff; in other cases a foundation may have no staff at all and be run by the founding family or volunteer trustees. In this book we refer to funders as having trustees and a staff, again to distinguish between the different roles in the grants process.

We assume that you have access to common office supplies and equipment such as a copier, computer with word processor, spreadsheet, and Internet access, as well as certain paper products. That's really all it takes to do a great job of grant seeking—that and the willingness to invest some time up front.

The time you will need to work your way through the book varies. The introductory chapters can be read in a single sitting. After that we estimate that following the book through from beginning to end, completing the exercises, and learning the system will take three weeks to three months, depending on your experience and how much time you have to dedicate to grant seeking. In any case we believe you'll start to see the benefits of the system well before you reach the end of the book, and the final results will more than repay your investment.

The two basic and most important assumptions this book makes are that your organization and program(s) are ready for grants and that you want to seek funding ethically. By "ready for grants" we mean that your organization is a 501(c)(3) nonprofit and is run somewhat efficiently and absolutely legally. We assume that the program for which you're fundraising fulfills a real need in the community and is planned to the point where you and your coworkers can answer some basic questions about it (which we'll cover in Chapter Four). Your nonprofit should be ready if it has dedicated volunteers, sound policies and planning, a CEO who is supportive of grant seeking, and a grasp of its goals and priorities for the next few years.

We also assume that you want to approach grant seeking as something other than a game in which you trick funders into giving up their cash or you twist the arms of the friends of your well-connected board members. Instead we assume your approach is based on openness, honesty about your good program and sound organization, and a bit of optimism.

Demystifying Grant Seeking

Prologue Get Inspired and Ready to Go

Clear Away Myths and Fears

Perhaps this sounds familiar. You're staying late—very late—at work the night before the proposal is due. Even the intern went home hours ago. You put on another pot of coffee and slog once again through the twenty pages you've written. Then you spend extra money to send the package by FedEx, the only way you can get the proposal in on time. You swear that after tonight you're not applying for any more grants. You just don't see how the few grants you get are worth this agony.

Or perhaps you supervise a staff person who handles grant writing, but he just doesn't seem to be getting that many checks in—or that many proposals in the mail for that matter. Perhaps he is caught up in other development projects, or his time is limited. You'd rather not nag him again about a grant resource he's neglecting to tap into. You wonder whether you will ever see results.

It doesn't have to be this way.

Grants are part of almost every nonprofit's world, whether your organization receives dozens of them or you are just beginning to wonder about them. Grants can be a substantial and meaningful funding source for many kinds of projects and organizations. And they can be a source of great hope and excitement.

At the same time few subjects in nonprofit management are surrounded by such fear and mystery. Few tasks are faced with such dread as writing and submitting grant proposals. Because you may never know why you do or don't get funded, it's common to look at grant funding as an irrational or chaotic process and grant makers as cruel or fickle.

Nonprofits that agonize over grant seeking act in accordance with these beliefs. When they hear about a grant opportunity, they scramble to design a program that fits the guidelines or work all night to get a confused proposal in the mail by the deadline. They conduct their grant seeking as an intermittent series of desperate gambles, which we call episodic grant seeking. The odds of success are poor. Nationally, only 1 to 10 percent of grant proposals are funded, according to a review in Dennis P. McIlnay's *How Foundations Work.*[1]

The effective grant seeker believes something completely different: that grant seeking and grant making are understandable and fairly rational processes. They run a steady, intelligent, fearless grant-seeking effort that minimizes work and pushes their odds well above the average. They do so by targeting the funders most compatible with their organization, by cultivating professional relationships with those funders, and by organizing their efforts for efficiency.

COMMON MYTHS ABOUT GRANTS AND GRANT SEEKING

This book gives you simple techniques you can use and habits you can develop to become an effective grant seeker. But before you try to apply them, you need to free yourself of some common misconceptions about grant seeking and get a more realistic idea of what you should and shouldn't expect from the process.

Myth: Grants are something for nothing.
Reality: Grants are rational deals
between colleagues.

Grants are appealing because they look like big chunks of free money. Unlike most individual donations, grants are often large enough to actually *buy* something, that is, to fund a whole program for an entire year or to purchase a major piece of equipment. And to get a grant you just send in an application. The funder sends back a check, and you don't need to pay it back. A grant seems like manna from heaven or a winning lottery ticket.

This perspective feeds some unfortunate practices and beliefs. Buying a lottery ticket takes no skill, so nonprofits that see grant seeking as gambling apply on impulse, without preparation; they assign the wrong people to work on proposals, or they place no value on the work of a skilled grant seeker. The only way they can increase their chances of winning a lottery is to buy more tickets, so some organizations practice the "spray and pray" method of grant seeking: sending out scores of identical proposals in hopes a few will "hit" and provide a windfall. Some nonprofits go fishing for funds, returning to the same foundations over and over again, hoping to eventually get a bite. Worse, some nonprofit staffers become sycophants, flattering grant makers and hoping this will provide an edge or an "in."

These methods are recipes for resentment and wasted labor. Rejections of desperate, heartfelt proposals naturally fuel the attitude that grant makers are fickle and unfair. Winning (or losing) a grant on the basis of flattery and connections rather than on the merits of the proposal can't do much but create a malaise that few at idealistic nonprofits will be comfortable with. And sending out scores of ill-considered proposals wastes a lot of work, not to mention paper and postage, considering that none are likely to be funded.

Grants are not free money. Foundations and other grant makers are organizations like your nonprofit. They have missions and goals just as you do. Funders award grants because what the grant recipients plan to do with the money fits in with the funders' own goals, initiatives, and dreams—and with their founder's stated wishes.

It makes sense to see a grant as a fair deal between colleagues whose interests are similar but whose resources are different. Your nonprofit and the funder have similar goals. One example might be housing the homeless. The funder has money to use for work toward that goal. Your nonprofit has the capability to do the work, with shelter space, expert staff, connections with health care providers, and so on. Your organization performs the work in exchange for the money. Your organization and its programs *have a value* that is equal to grant money.

If you can recognize this value, you will stop praying, fishing, and flattering for grants. You will begin to look for and see matches with funders whose interests and goals are most like yours. You will behave less like a supplicant or gambler and more like a *partner* with funders. You will handle rejection better, too, because you will be able to conceive that it is possible that some other organization had a proposal that fit the funder's goals just as well as yours.

Acknowledging the full value of your own organization and its programs isn't always easy. Grant seekers and grant makers are bound up in a status relationship so deeply ingrained it is sometimes difficult to recognize. Grant seekers are accustomed to—even proud of—being poor, fighting for recognition and justice, and having to beg for money. They have a lower status than grant makers, who often play the part of exclusive or "noble" organizations.

This status difference seems to come from a belief that money (or the ability to give it away) is more respectable than expertise, ability, or action. It hasn't helped that some funders have been willing to take on a superior role, hiding behind unlisted phone numbers or gatekeepers and making forbidding statements like one we heard recently: "Dr. X prefers not to meet with anyone." At one workshop we attended, a program officer from a well-known national foundation seemed to admit his organization found ambiguity convenient when he said, "It is the policy of the foundation to not be comfortable with getting too clear."

The pecking order is perpetuated every day when nonprofits flatter and supplicate in their grant seeking. They are just as complicit as funders, coming to believe they are "owed something" for their good work. They attempt to play their low status to their advantage, appealing to those higher up with their incredible need and devotion. Some grants consultants might advocate that you adopt this role. But no matter how we in the nonprofit world martyr ourselves for the good of our causes, funders are free to make their own decisions.

Although it is unproductive to demand or expect to be funded just because foundations "have to give it away," it might empower you to remember that a funder's money can do little good for the community unless it is invested, for example, in organizations like yours. Funders need nonprofits to spend their money effectively just as much as nonprofits need funders to pay for their programs.

It's also encouraging to remember that although grant seeking seems surrounded by mystery, it is basically a rational process. Usually some or all of the criteria used to award a grant are presented in writing, and if you are not awarded a grant, you may be able to find out why. Often it is because your organization did not fit the written guidelines or the unwritten but discernable priorities of the foundation trustees.

That's not to say grant making is 100 percent fair. Even fair deals between colleagues involve some intangible elements like trust, and any process involving money is open to misunderstanding and corruption. Even at the fairest of trustee meetings, very good programs and proposals can end up as the least important ones on the table.

Still you have control over many elements of the process: which funders you apply to, how you relate to those funders, which information you present to them, how you present it, and how you organize your efforts. Efficient grant seekers raise more money in less time because they take charge of these parts of the process—the parts they can control—rather than leaving them to vagaries of flattery, hope, or luck.

Myth: Writing grant proposals is an ordeal.
Reality: Proposal writing is predictable and simple.

Although the specific requirements of grant makers vary, and your proposals should be tailored for each funder, all grant applications involve just *one basic activity:* responding to a set of questions about your nonprofit organization and its programs. This set of questions varies little from funder to funder. A few you'll see again and again include: Who and how many people will be served by program X? How will the effectiveness of program Y be evaluated? What other organizations do you collaborate with? What other funds have you sought?

If you know your organization and its programs well, answering these questions will be a fairly straightforward process. The experience of grant writing as an ordeal—staying up all night, agonizing, and racing the envelope to FedEx at the last second—comes not from the nature of grant seeking but from predictable situations at nonprofits that are desperate for money but ill-prepared to answer key questions. Presented with a grant opportunity, some nonprofits try to design whole new projects from scratch at the last second so they can apply with something that fits the funding requirements. We strongly object to this practice on the grounds of both practicality and principle.

In purely logistical terms, designing a new program is naturally hard work that takes a long time and must be done *before the questions in a grant proposal can be answered.* It's work most appropriately done by an organization's *program staff,* who are the experts on day-to-day operations. An experienced member of the *development staff,* such as yourself, might have skills in spotting good programs and be able to help design new ones, but you never want to invent a new program without the cooperation of program staff. You could get funded for a program that is not ready to roll and have serious trouble following through. You might even have to return the money.

Or you might raise the money, your organization might follow through, and you'd "get away" with it. This can create what nonprofit managers call mission creep, that is, when your mission changes due to external factors such as money. Why would you want to be involved in such a transaction? If you're like many fundraisers, you got involved in nonprofits because you really believed in a cause or program. We think you should hang on to that idealism and use it as your guiding star rather than pursue funding for funding's sake or create bureaucracies that no one believes in.

A better way to operate is for you, the grant seeker, to ask the program staff basic questions about your organization and relevant programs and use their answers to write grant proposals. If the program staff have trouble answering the kinds of questions foundations often ask, they probably need to think through their ideas or document their experience more carefully before they ask you to write a proposal. As you become experienced with grant seeking, your role as development staff should be to help program planners ask themselves the right questions. (Chapter Four contains exercises to help both development and program staff collect the answers you'll need to know before applying for any grant.)

When you know your organization well, and programs are fully designed and ready for grant seeking, the actual writing of grant proposals turns out to be easy. After creating a few of them, you'll notice that although the order or wording of the questions may vary from funder to funder, the questions themselves are very much the same.

The requirements of grant applications are repetitive and predictable. As a consequence, making an investment in preparation and organization will speed the writing and assembling of all your proposals. Several chapters in this book describe how you can anticipate needs and have much of the necessary material ready before you even think of applying to any particular funder.

In fact grant seeking involves so much organization and preparation and so many clerical tasks that it is more trouble than it's worth to apply for one or two grants. If you make an investment of time in setting up a grant-seeking system, you can easily apply for ten or twenty grants instead of one. And if you make a steady, consistent effort, even if it is low key, chances are that your investment will eventually pay off. You'll be left with more time to spend any way you want: on the finer points of each proposal, on your other job duties, or on sleep.

*Myth: All you need is one well-written
grant proposal.
Reality: Winning grants depends on pinpointing
matches and tailoring proposals.*

As consultants we have been approached by many nonprofit organizations, each asking us to write a single "boilerplate" proposal that can be sent out to many funders. This is the kind of job we don't take because a single grant proposal is right only for the funder for which it is written, and sending it to dozens of funders at once is usually a waste of resources. Grant makers can tell when they've been sent a form letter, and it likely makes them feel just about as special as you do when you get a letter from Ed McMahon.

Grant proposals all have similar elements, and a handful of funders even accept Common Grant Application forms, which save administrative time for applicants. However, every proposal, even one submitted on a common form, should have at *least* a cover letter that points out how the program in question specifically matches with the funder's mission and goals. As a grant seeker you will spend time making crucial decisions about what we call matches, that is, which programs you will present to which funders and for how much funding. Sending a boilerplate proposal skips over the important steps of matching the potential funder with your program and presenting the match in a way that the particular funder will find pertinent and compelling. It also skips over the brief but essential task of updating your text with the most recent changes in your program goals and community trends, which can lend a sense of timeliness and relevance to your proposal.

*Myth: You need to "know someone" to get a grant.
Reality: You don't need to know anyone to start, and
relationships can be built as you go.*

One Monday morning two years ago we observed an otherwise rational program director come into a weekly staff meeting in a state of tremendous excitement.

Over the weekend he had been best man at a wedding where he had met the *brother-in-law of a trustee from a big foundation!* He thought this personal contact had won a crucial "in" for our organization, regardless of the fact that we didn't even meet the foundation's guidelines for funding.

Many people have heard that relationships are crucial to foundation fundraising; in general that is true. However, the crucial relationships in steady, systematic grant seeking aren't personal friendships. They are business relationships built on confidence and mutual regard—the elements necessary to work together in a significant way. Consider how you might react if someone asked you for a dime for their project. You'd probably give ten cents to anyone, stranger or friend, without much thought or expectation. But if someone asked you for a thousand dollars, you might reasonably wonder what kind of track record the person had, whether you could trust him or her to follow through, and how success or failure might reflect on you.

Similarly, many small grants (and once in a while a large one) are awarded with zero personal contact and no preexisting relationships. We had the experience of starting from scratch with an organization that had minimal business relationships with foundations, and we raised 10 percent of that organization's budget through grants in our first year there, working entirely through the mail.

For larger or more significant grants you will need relationships, but you can initiate and cultivate them in a businesslike way. You might be introduced to foundation staff or trustees through public knowledge of your program's work, a personal introduction by a trusted colleague, or a record of successful use of prior grant funds. For example, you may have gotten small grants through the mail. These elementary relationships can be crucial because they provide an accepted context in which to build up positive background information about your organization before the next funding decision is made. Assuming you have a good program, it's likely that the better a grant maker knows you the more they will trust you as a steward of their funds.

An efficient grant seeker sends a steady stream of good information to funders without going overboard. You want to develop an evolving relationship of collaboration in which you consistently provide proof that your organization is a responsible and effective partner in a potential funder's efforts. Such relationships can position your organization to be a serious contender for very significant grants.

This kind of relationship, more than a chat with someone's brother-in-law, will ultimately be your "in."

Myth: Grants are too inconsistent to deserve
the attention of fundraising staff.
Reality: Grants are consistently useful for
certain projects and needs.

It is true that foundation grants make up a relatively small percentage of overall giving in the United States. In 1998 they accounted for slightly less than 10 percent of all gifts to charity, according to the American Association of Fund Raising Counsel. In contrast, individual donations accounted for 77 percent.[2]

In addition to grants being a small piece of the pie, there are a few disadvantages to relying on them. For example, if you are balancing your organization's livelihood on one big grant, your organization could fall if that grant gets used up or withdrawn. Having a large grant early in its life cycle can catapult an organization through all the difficulties of a slow grassroots start-up, but it can just as easily lead an organization to delude itself about the kind of fundraising it needs to do. Several times we have been contacted by organizations that were founded with a single large grant, asking us to seek new grants just as their founding money was about to run out. In one case only six months remained before their entire bank account would be emptied, but their experience led them to believe that a foundation would swoop in from out of state and pay for everything, including the heating bill.

It is difficult to bear bad news, but you will find that one of your most important jobs as a grant seeker is to educate people about the reality of grants: how long they take to get, what they're good for, and how they should fit in with other kinds of fundraising. Large grants, especially from national funders, can take over a year to prepare and receive. Given current foundation giving patterns and initiatives, there are fewer and fewer national foundations even accepting unsolicited proposals, and they simply won't pay for many things.

Under current foundation practices, grants are most often given to the following: to start up new projects, make major expansions to existing projects, replicate successful projects in new locations, meet one-time capital or program needs, build an organization's internal capacity to carry out its mission, and fund innovative communitywide initiatives and partnerships that join several nonprofit organizations or sectors.

This means that some important areas of need at your organization will never (under normal circumstances) be paid for by a grant. These may include administrative staffing, maintenance of buildings, insurance, and ongoing expenses for a successful program that is not changing, expanding, or spinning off in any way. In addition, foundations rarely fund conferences, publications, or programs that benefit only a few individuals. Applying for grants for these items on their own, without their being an integral part of a larger project that fits current foundation giving guidelines, will nearly always be a waste of time.

With a few exceptions (such as "small grant" or "minigrant" programs), foundations do not want to be the sole funder of a program or project. They prefer to see you seeking a base of support that includes a range of sources, from other foundations to individuals.

Neither do funders want your organization to become overly reliant on them over the long term. They tend not to make commitments beyond two- or three-year grant periods; many will not even consider a grant request that goes beyond one year. Each grant you receive will likely be made for something temporary such as a new beginning, significant expansion, new building or van, renovated roof, or one-time special project. This is another reason we advocate a regular grant-seeking effort. We want to ensure that when you do have *new* projects and *specific* needs, you have a system to bring them in front of your foundation donors, asking them to "re-up" their giving by focusing on something new.

Even when your organization is a good candidate for grants, they can rarely, if ever, be all the funding you need. In many established organizations grants are less than 10 percent of their total income, excluding years when they have special campaigns such as capital building projects. For most organizations, having a large number of individual donors is especially important. Individual donations tend to be unrestricted (you can use them for whatever you deem your highest priority), and the process of getting an individual donation can be relatively quick—a phone call or a letter. We've assisted in a few phone bank efforts for struggling arts organizations and have been impressed with their effectiveness, as thousands of dollars were raised by a small team of volunteers in just a few hours. In contrast a grant can take six to twelve months to come in after a proposal is mailed. So you won't want to seek grants for an emergency need or program that is slated to start in one month.

So what *is* the point of spending time on grant seeking? Even given their limitations, grants can be a significant source of revenue for your nonprofit. There are most likely several projects or outstanding needs at your organization that *do* fit foundation giving patterns and for which you need substantial funding. Your strategy will be to focus on these and recommend that other needs be supported by other kinds of fundraising.

Myth: Grants are few, huge, and national.
Reality: Grants are most often small, numerous,
and local.

Media coverage of grants might lead anyone to believe that grants are few and far between but that when they happen they are tremendous. So if grants are gigantic pieces of money that are given by well-known foundations and that only touch your community once in a blue moon, why would you want to launch an organized, year-round, grant-seeking effort?

The reality is that for most organizations, grants are medium-sized gifts that come from the same local and regional foundations every year. When we started grant writing, we were surprised and excited to learn from the *Oregon Foundation Data Book* that there were more than 280 foundations—unsung family and corporate foundations as well as major philanthropic institutions—in our home state of Oregon.[3] It turned out that we could conduct an entire grant-seeking effort, appropriate for a regional nonprofit, without once thinking of applying to the Rockefeller, Carnegie, or Pew organizations. After a few years we began to identify times when it was appropriate to approach national funders, but they were never our primary focus as grant seekers for small nonprofits with local programs and budgets under $1 million.

We have found it useful to divide grant opportunities into two general types: bread-and-butter grants, which are recurring (often annual) opportunities, usually from local or regional sources, and icing-on-the-cake grants, which are large, often one-time opportunities.

Most nonprofits are small or medium-sized organizations that operate local or regional programs, and throughout this book we assume you are among this majority. There are likely to be an abundance of bread-and-butter local and regional funders available to you, and with rare exceptions this is where you should concentrate your grant seeking. Similar to the effect of expanding your list of individual donors, this approach moves your organization toward a broader base of funding; if one or two funders are lost, your organization will still have many others, and you won't be scrambling to raise money when your one big grant runs out. Bread-and-butter grants also provide an opportunity to increase grant income year after year. As long as your proposals are well thought out, you may be able to apply to the same local foundations year after year with different projects and requests. This way you slowly build relationships of collaboration and trust.

Icing-on-the-cake, super grants should be approached only occasionally, that is, when your organization fits the guidelines and the opportunity seems very strong. For example, a major computer company might send out a special RFP (request for proposals), announcing the giveaway of millions of dollars in equipment for organizations exactly like yours and in your geographic area. Or you might have a truly innovative project that deserves the attention of a foundation with a national scope and mandate. If your request fits the guidelines, and your program has elements that make it stand out among the hundreds of proposals that are received each week at a typical national foundation, you may rise to the top and be given serious consideration. You may be asked for a site visit; you might even ultimately receive a grant. But this scenario is very rare for a local or regional program.

Myth: Taking grant funding means selling out your program.
Reality: You control your programs, and you can select donors that fit with your mission.

As we mentioned, the ill-prepared or episodic grant seeker may struggle to create a program that fits the guidelines of a specific funder when a big grant opportunity arises. Or an organization might approach grant seeking only when it's financially desperate and willing to take any and all suggestions from funders, hoping that if they comply they'll get funded. It's not surprising that anyone who goes about grant seeking this way, or who has seen others do so, might believe a nonprofit has to sell its soul or corrupt its mission to accept foundation funding.

It is not necessary to work this way. If you conduct a steady, year-round grant-seeking effort, you gain control over the process. You select whom you will approach as a potential funder, based on any criteria you wish, and you select how much funding you'll ask for and when. Because you don't wait until you're financially desperate, you start from a position of more power, able to decide whether a funding opportunity is worth any requirements it may come with. Proceeding with integrity lets you protect your identity and ideals. You also come across as a more stable organization, ready and able to handle grant funding.

When you do receive grants from the funders you have chosen to work with (and for programs that make sense given your mission and goals), you may find you have little to worry about regarding selling out. What we've found is that foundations most often require little more than a good, solid program. They don't often ask for (or sometimes even desire) broad recognition of their grants unless they are affiliated with corporations. Most local or regional foundations that are smaller than the Pews and Gateses usually leave program evaluation up to the grant seeker, asking that you report to them once per year using your own criteria for program success.

The key to maintaining the integrity of your programs lies in your choices about whom you apply to and how you work. If you seek grants and other funding consistently, you won't need to twist and turn your organization just to get money.

WHAT YOU CAN EXPECT

Now that you've dispensed with some of the most pernicious myths about grant seeking, you are ready to jump start an effective grant-seeking effort. To get started and get grants, you don't need to stay up all night and write like a nonprofit Shakespeare. You don't need to introduce yourself to the entire civic elite of your town. What you need is not fortitude, connections, or eloquence. You need a system. Along with a new attitude about grants, a system will carry you through months and years of productive grant seeking. This book will show you one system that works. Think of it as a guide for your next few months; exercises and worksheets will point you on your way.

Don't be surprised if you feel frustrated at first. Like most skills, effective grant seeking has a learning curve, and there are not many substitutes for putting in time reading and writing. You can expect to make a considerable investment of your time in research and in filing before you write a single word of a grant proposal.

Our philosophy is about *minimizing* work through consistency and simplicity. Stick with us, and you will only have to do many of these activities once. Other tasks are repetitive but will become easier and faster as time goes on. By the end of the book, you'll have more than a few grant proposals in the mail. You'll have your own complete grant-seeking system to speed and enhance all your future work.

Understand the Grant-Seeking Cycle

Every serious grant seeker, whether part-time volunteer or full-time consultant, goes through the same basic cycle of activities. To use your time effectively you need to recognize the steps in the cycle and plan accordingly. In this chapter we'll describe those steps (see Figure 2.1). Because this book takes you through the complete cycle once, learning the steps also gives you a preview of where the book is going.

As we see it, five phases are involved with every grant request. The step you might think of as the end of the process—writing and delivering the grant proposal—we see as just one task in the middle of an ongoing cycle of learning and developing relationships.

STEP ONE: LEARN

First you need to learn about three subjects: (1) your organization's needs and strengths, (2) your community and its needs, and (3) your potential funders and their goals. Any grant proposal must demonstrate a basic compatibility among these three essential ingredients.

STEP TWO: MATCH

Next match your organization's programs and needs with a particular funder's giving patterns and mission. Out of your organization's many needs determine which

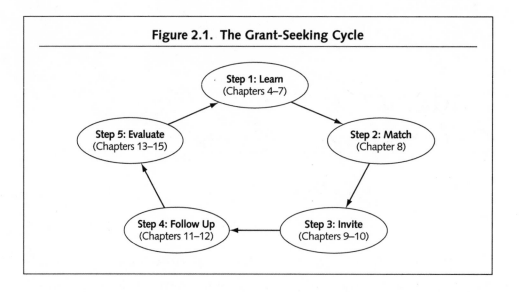

Figure 2.1. The Grant-Seeking Cycle

- Step 1: Learn (Chapters 4–7)
- Step 2: Match (Chapter 8)
- Step 3: Invite (Chapters 9–10)
- Step 4: Follow Up (Chapters 11–12)
- Step 5: Evaluate (Chapters 13–15)

ones the funder will find most interesting. Your goal is to move beyond a mere compatibility with a funder to discover the specific things the funder will find compelling and natural to support. Now you know exactly what you will ask for.

STEP THREE: INVITE

Next invite the funder to invest in your organization by giving you a grant. You might make this invitation by writing a full grant proposal, but the invitation could begin with a simple phone call, letter of inquiry, or face-to-face meeting.

STEP FOUR: FOLLOW UP

Making the invitation is not the end of the process. Follow-up is essential. Within your organization you need to keep people informed about the process and involved in it. With the funder you need to respond to the result of your invitation, whether the result is a check in the mail, an invitation to submit a full proposal, a request for a visit to see your program in action, or a flat-out rejection. Keep the funder engaged, and cultivate a collegial relationship—one worthy of fair deals between equals.

STEP FIVE: EVALUATE

Finally, evaluate how all the previous steps worked and how your methods can be improved. Why did you or didn't you get the grant? It is often possible to find out. Was your work efficient enough to make getting the grant worthwhile? What are your next opportunities, and how should you pursue them? Armed with this self-knowledge, head into Step One again, ready to learn about any changes in your program, your community, and your next prospective funder's mission before you invite them to invest in your organization.

HOW THE CYCLE WORKS

An example may give you a picture of how the cycle works. Imagine you are a grant seeker for a social service nonprofit that operates free health clinics.

You fulfill Step One by gathering information about your organization's health clinics. You find out, for example, what part of the community they serve and what sort of equipment they need to buy. You learn about the funders in your region who are interested in health issues.

In Step Two you use the information you've gathered to zero in on a funder that has a history of funding local health projects. You decide to ask that funder for money to purchase an expensive piece of equipment.

Once you have made a match in your mind and on paper, you can carry out Step Three by calling the foundation to introduce yourself and responding when you are asked to send a written grant proposal.

Once your proposal is mailed, you move immediately into Step Four by communicating with your board of directors and your colleagues about the request you sent. You also call to invite the foundation representatives to tour your clinic. When you receive a grant for your clinic, follow up with the funder by sending an official note of thanks and by scheduling future progress reports and reminders to keep your program fresh in the funder's mind.

Finally, you can move into Step Five; you look over your work with this funder and plan for any adjustments. For example, perhaps the foundation staff mentioned to you that they'd like to see a more detailed budget next time, so you decide to spruce up your financial documents before applying for any more grants.

Now you are ready to work on the next grant proposal for the next prospective funder. You circle back to Step One, where you find out that there are a few changes to your health clinic's goals for the coming year, and you also begin researching your next funding lead.

HOW TIMING IN THE CYCLE VARIES

In this book we take you through the cycle one complete time, giving detailed exercises for each step. The time and effort required your first time through depends on how many hours per week you work, your experience with grants, and other factors. It may take one to three months. After the first time you will go through the cycle much faster, sometimes taking as little as two days.

This book assumes you're just beginning your serious grant-seeking work, so we anticipate that you'll spend the most time on Step One, as you absorb a great deal of information about your organization, community, and funders, and set up systems like your electronic and paper files. This can be hard work. That's why it takes up four chapters of the book. But much of what you learn will be relevant to all your future grant proposals. If your first grant proposal seems to be taking a while to prepare for, remember that you won't have to do Step One in such detail again.

After the first time through, moving around the cycle becomes easier and easier, and the way you budget your time will evolve. Even on your second time through the cycle you'll reap the rewards of good preparation, as Step One takes considerably less time. By your fifth time around, learning may be as quick as brushing up on any changes in your program's annual service goals or downloading a current application form from a funder's Web site. Still, because the world changes, you'll never completely eliminate the job of learning, as one cynical grant seeker observed when he complained that improvements in the program he worked for kept messing up his boilerplate proposal.

As you get more proposals out in the mail and more grant funding coming into your organization, Step Four will occupy more of your time. You will be cultivating all those new relationships and collaborations your work has initiated. When you become even more experienced with grant seeking, and your organization and programs are well known to local and regional funders, you'll start to focus much of your effort on Step Three, asking for more meetings with funders and inviting them to tour your program and invest in it at more significant levels. Finally, a year or two from now, if your organization invents a new program or plans a capital campaign, you may find yourself spending more time on Step One again, learning all the details of the new venture.

WHAT'S NEXT

Now that you know something about the theory and cyclical nature of grant seeking, it's time to get down to work. Before we dive into Step One, we'll have some fun ordering office supplies.

Set Up a Simple Office

Now that you've prepared yourself mentally, dispensed with the myths about grants, and learned about the steps involved in grant seeking, it's time to start building the staging area for your five-step cycle. In this chapter you'll learn to set up your office space.

Mostly what you'll be doing is making empty file folders that will be filled in as you work through the rest of this book. It's simple but not at all trivial work, because each element of the office space, including each file folder, *physically reflects* some important aspect of effective grant seeking. We'll explain the function and significance of each element as we go along.

Your office space and files are critical because one of your main tasks as an effective grant seeker is to be a master of information. You gather it, synthesize it, and make it available to funders and coworkers in the right format at the right time. You need an office and a set of files that keeps it all in order so you don't get overwhelmed and the process doesn't bog down.

You'll build your sophisticated information processing system out of low-tech office supplies like file folders and index cards. Although you'll need a computer for word processing, searching the Internet, and so on, we discourage buying or creating a special computer database to hold your files or track your grant-seeking efforts, at least for now. For most readers a new database would take a significant investment of money and time, and it isn't needed to get started.

Our low-tech system was created at a small nonprofit, but it transferred successfully to work at one of the biggest charities in the Pacific Northwest (The Salvation Army, Cascade Division). It's accurate and inexpensive, and it will never crash at an inopportune moment. Perhaps most important is that your key files will be readily understandable and accessible, not just to you but to your coworkers. If it makes it more glamorous to do so, think of this paper system as voluntary simplicity.

DO YOU HAVE TO FOLLOW THIS SYSTEM EXACTLY?

In this chapter we start giving you detailed instructions about things to do. You might wonder whether instead of following the directions exactly you should branch off and start making your own variation on the system right away. The answer is an emphatic *no,* at least for the time being.

Our experience teaching this system to clients has shown that although it doesn't really matter if you use, say, regular file folders instead of hanging file folders, following the details exactly will make it easier for you to follow the book. You won't be translating back and forth all the time. More importantly, the functions of some parts of the system will become more understandable *once you have practiced using them.* Only after you've gotten to the end of the book and used the system enough to understand how and why each part really works is it a good idea to deviate. Then you can customize our system until you create the system of your dreams.

Your organization might already have a set of grant-related files. You should ignore them for the time being and pretend you're a beginner. If you're really in good shape, you'll breeze through the rest of the book anyway. But if your files are less than orderly, you will be able to start anew by following the book. You can move your existing materials into the new system later.

MATERIALS AND SPACE

Figure 3.1 shows a sketch of all the office you'll ever need to raise millions of dollar in grants. As you can see, no mahogany desk or leather chair is required.

To get started:

➔ Claim a work space big enough to call your own.

The space can be as limited as a small desk plus a file cabinet. If you have to share a desk, you will need three file drawers at least. If you have any say in the mat-

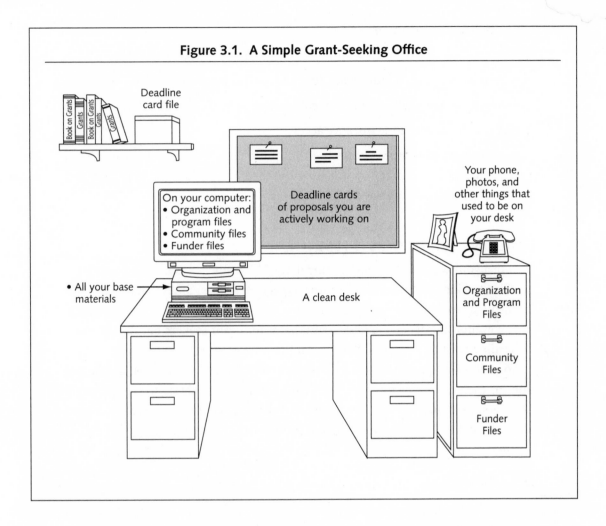

Figure 3.1. A Simple Grant-Seeking Office

Deadline card file

Book on Grants
Grants
Book on Grants
Grants

On your computer:
• Organization and program files
• Community files
• Funder files

Deadline cards of proposals you are actively working on

Your phone, photos, and other things that used to be on your desk

• All your base materials

A clean desk

Organization and Program Files

Community Files

Funder Files

ter, consider the location of your desk or cubicle or office carefully. A private or secluded spot is desirable because at times you will need to work without interruption.

→ Gather the following resources:

- About thirty hanging file folders to start with

- File folder labels

- An index card file with blank index cards and twelve dividers labeled with the months of the year

- A bulletin board and pushpins

- Access to a photocopier, with white and colored copy paper

- Your organization's letterhead (first and second pages and envelopes)

- A bookcase or shelf to store current research materials

- A telephone with long distance access

- A computer with word processing and spreadsheet programs, Internet access, and access to a printer. You will also need the free computer program, Acrobat Reader, available at www.adobe.com.

DEADLINE TRACKING SYSTEM

Now that your workspace is full of shiny new office supplies, it's time to create your deadline tracking system, which is a way to keep all the deadlines you'll encounter in one place so you and other people won't be caught unaware by them. Anticipating events and needs is a very useful habit for grant seekers because it minimizes time-wasting surprises. You'll see it mentioned often in this book.

Your deadline tracking system will be simple: a box of index cards, with a section for each month of the year. Each card will hold one deadline, for example "XYZ Foundation, proposals due, June 15." A deadline card can represent any kind of deadline: the date a proposal is due, the date you need to make an important call, and so on.

→ Put the index card file box on your shelf in a clearly visible place.

→ Make twelve dividers to put in the box, one for each month. Don't put years on the dividers because you can anticipate that the same deadlines will occur year after year, and you will work in cycles, reusing materials whenever you can.

→ Hang the bulletin board on the wall in a clearly visible place.

In the future you will be using the deadline system this way: periodically (perhaps once a week) you will flip through the deadline cards, see which deadlines are approaching, and decide which ones you will work on. Then you will stick those cards on the bulletin board, making them "active," to remind yourself that you need to work on that material. After you've met a deadline, you'll put the card back in the box for next year.

This deadline system, though low-tech, functions nicely in several ways. Most important, it keeps deadlines constantly visible (unlike electronic reminders that flash on the screen temporarily). It reinforces the choices you've made to focus on a few specific projects that are likely to bear fruit, and, unlike your day planner, it's in public view. When your coworkers come in and distract you with unwelcome chatter or griping, you can point at the deadline cards and beg off gracefully.

ESSENTIAL FILES

You need at least three file drawers because you'll be dealing with three types of information, that is, information about your community, your organization, and your funders. Now we'll proceed to fill those three drawers with all the file folders you'll need to begin.

➔ First label your three drawers "Organization and Program Files," "Community Files," and "Funder Files," respectively.

Organization and Program Files

You can't do a good job of grant seeking without knowing your own organization and its programs well. Once you do gain this knowledge, you'll need to refer to it again and again.

➔ Create file folders with the following labels, and put them in the drawer you labeled "Organization and Program Files" (they'll remain empty right now; just create them):

- Organizational resume
- Board list
- Bios of key people
- 501(c)(3) letter
- Organizational budget for current year
- Current financial statement
- Last two audited financial statements (two separate folders)
- Most recent IRS form 990

- By-laws
- Antidiscrimination policy
- Letters of support
- Newspaper clippings
- Stories

Grants are most often for programs or projects, rarely for general operating expenses. You'll need to become an expert on the specific programs and projects your organization operates and is planning to operate. Therefore you'll need a few more files.

→ Using the information in Chapter One about what grants are often given for, decide on one or two projects or programs for which you will be seeking grant money. An example might be "public education campaign." Write the project names here:

✍ Project 1: _____

✍ Project 2: _____

Then do this:

→ Make one file folder for each of these projects, and put them in the drawer empty.

Take a moment to consider the topics these files represent. Pieces of information like your board list, letters of support, and simple descriptions of your organization's projects will be the base materials of every grant proposal you create. After you've filled these files (in Chapters Four through Seven), you will find that writing grants is mostly a matter of combining these materials.

Paper Files Versus Computer Files

As you might have imagined, some of your paper file folders will be filled with documents you create on your computer. It makes sense to keep those documents saved on the computer for ready reference (along with templates for things like budgets and blocks of text that recur in all your grant proposals, as we'll describe later). Still, our experience shows us that you will save time and trouble by having the paper versions printed and filed because, as of this writing, most foundations only accept proposals on paper. It makes sense to keep your computer files divided up in the same way as your paper files. So do this:

→ Create computer folders for "Community," "Organization and Program," and "Funders." You will start filling them soon.

Community Files

An essential part of successful grant seeking is understanding and expressing the need that your community—be it your neighborhood, town, state, country, or planet—has for the services your organization provides. You will be creating and maintaining a small library that documents this subject. To start your library out, do the following:

→ Create paper file folders with the following labels, and put them in the drawer you marked "Community Files":
  • Press clippings
  • Anecdotes
  • Statistics
  • Published reports
  • Newsletters and materials from other nonprofits
  • Any other community-related files you want to make

→ Create similar folders on your computer as subfolders, under "Community." You may also want to create a folder for community links in your World Wide Web browser's bookmark menu.

Funder Files

You will be collecting and processing a great deal of information about the funders that make grants. You will need to understand and control this information and keep it accessible. In the future you will create one file folder for each funder that you research or work with, and these will go in the drawer you marked "Funder Files." Each funder file will contain all your information about and correspondence with that funder. To get the system started, do this:

→ Think about three funders that you are interested in or involved with, and write their names in the blanks provided. An example might be Smith Foundation.

🖎 Funder 1: _____

🖎 Funder 2: _____

🖎 Funder 3: _____

→ Create three file folders labeled with the funders' names, and put them in the drawer empty.

→ Then do something important: sort these files in the drawer in alphabetical order by funder name.

All of this filing, especially alphabetizing three files, may seem rather compulsive, but you need to get into the right habits to control the flow of information in your office. Eventually you may have hundreds of funder files, and you're not organizing them just for yourself. Other people at your organization will have to find material in your files, especially if you work part-time or you're a volunteer. Your filing system has to be self-explanatory because you may not be in the office when an important call comes in from a foundation representative.

Whenever you add a funder file to the drawer, you should create a corresponding folder in your computer, inside the folder that you labeled "Funders." You will eventually have many of these, which will arrange themselves alphabetically for you with the click of a mouse.

Special Files

Your Organization and Program, Community, and Funder files will make up the majority of your file system. But you need a few more special file folders to hold information that's in flux.

Open up your "Organization and Program Files" drawer again. Create four more empty hanging files, and drop them in at the front of this drawer. They should be labeled this way:

- "To Read and Consider"
- "Funders to Contact"
- "Folders to Make"
- "Grant Tracking"

You need the first three special files so you can follow another habit of effective grant seekers: dividing your work time into blocks. New information will be coming in to you all the time. It can be a distraction to try to comprehend it when you're in the middle of something else, like writing a proposal. Drop incoming material in "To Read and Consider" and leave it there until the time you schedule for reading. "Funders to Contact" and "Folders to Make" serve similar functions, which we'll explain later.

The last folder, "Grant Tracking," won't have many pages in it, just a simple, ongoing record of the proposals you've sent out and how they fared. We'll cover this in Chapter Eleven.

CONGRATULATIONS

You're already on your way to more effective grant seeking. Now that your files are made, you're ready to fill them up and use them as the nerve center of your five-step process.

Learn About Your
Organization,
Community,
and Funders

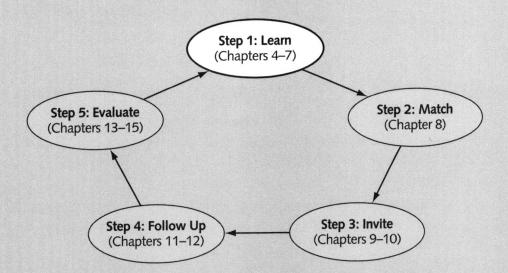

You need to learn about three subjects: (1) your organization's
needs and strengths, (2) your community and its needs, and
(3) your potential funders and their goals. Any grant proposal
must demonstrate a basic compatibility among these three
essential ingredients.

Learn About Your Organization and Programs

It's time to roll up your sleeves and start filling your file cabinet with the material that will become the foundation of your grant proposals. In this chapter you'll answer essential questions about your organization and its programs, both current and planned. These will be questions about your organization's identity and purpose: Why does it exist? What does it do? Why is it important in the larger scheme of things? These are exactly the kind of questions you will need to answer in grant proposals.

As a grant seeker you don't invent the answers to these questions. Rather, as we'll show you in this chapter, you go straight to the sources who are most knowledgeable and get the answers from them. Then in the next chapter you'll use your skill as a writer and synthesizer of information to express those answers in a clear and compelling way.

Some of the questions we want you to address are basic, and if you work for an organization that is at all established, many will be answered already in brochures, annual reports, or previous grant proposals. Your organization may even have a case statement, that is, a document written to state the case for supporting your cause, which most often contains information similar to what's needed for grant seeking. All these kinds of documents are important ingredients in your learning process, and you should certainly collect and read them.

However, collecting and reading is no substitute for asking questions of knowledgeable people. In interviews you may be able to comprehend the real meaning of existing texts (which aren't always well written). Just as important, you will probably dig up information that isn't printed anywhere but could be valuable for writing compelling grant proposals.

An example can demonstrate the value of the personal interview. Grant makers almost always ask why, how, and when your organization was founded. In our work with an innovative arts organization, we found their files contained many documents that included the facts of their founding, and we could easily have written a standard response for the funders we were approaching. It probably would have read something like this:

> The Orlo Foundation is a nonprofit organization dedicated to exploring environmental issues through the creative arts. Founded by a group of artists in 1991, our organization has operated for nine years in Portland.

However, we sat down with a long-time board member of the organization and asked him questions about Orlo's founding. Because we were talking with him in person, we were able to push for details. We asked him for the *story* of how the organization was started. Ultimately we came up with this answer for potential funders:

> In 1991, painter Philip Krohn took the lead in organizing a group of artists who had concerns about environmental issues, and who envisioned an organization that would combine their passions. Krohn's family had spent a lot of time in central Oregon, among the big trees, and to honor his family's love of the land he provided startup funding for the organization they envisioned—an organization that would use art to explore environmental themes, to get past divisive politics and communicate deeply about frightening ecological problems. Krohn found a supportive landlord to give a discount on a space in Portland's Northwest Industrial Area. The Orlo Foundation is still operating in that space today, pursuing the mission laid out nine years ago by our founders.

We'd venture that the second version is far more compelling. Besides the required facts about founding date and operating location, it gives potential funders a sense of the spirit and vision of the organization. Including such details and using that kind of storytelling can really make your grant proposal stand out, as you'll discover when you get to Step Three of the grant-seeking cycle. We never would have been able to write this more interesting version without a face-to-face meeting.

YOUR ORGANIZATION

To learn about your organization, start at the top. You need to talk to the person who is both knowledgeable about the organization and empowered to direct it day to day.

→ Make an appointment with your CEO. You will need one to two hours of his or her time. Write the time and date in here:

 _____

During this meeting, you will have a very specific goal: to get or learn how to get answers to a number of questions about where your organization came from and where it is going. Although the questions are described in detail in this chapter, they are also listed in Exhibit A.1 (in Resource A). Take a copy of this list to your interview, and use it to guide your conversation.

This isn't a public interview, so there's no need to be overly formal about it. You're having a general conversation about your whole organization and its activities, not any one specific program or project. As you listen and take notes, start thinking about how to express the answer to each question in direct, compelling language that any intelligent person—not just someone in your field—could understand and be moved by. Try to move your conversation beyond the language of your organization's official mission statement and printed documents.

Mission and Style

Potential funders will always ask you to briefly describe the general background and purpose of your organization. The ways this might be phrased on a grant application form vary from a simple "description of agency"[1] to a more specific "short description of the organization, including its legal name, history, activities, purpose and governing board."[2] In addition, funders will want to know about the community need your organization addresses. A funder may ask you to describe "community needs and strengths"[3] or "evidence showing a need for the program."[4]

To prepare for writing those parts of grant proposals, you should ask your CEO questions like these:

✔ When, why, and how did our organization start? Exactly who founded our organization?

✔ What is the story of our founding? Was it in response to a critical need or incident?

✔ What is the community need that we address? How is this need important to our community? Do we address the need on a local, regional, state, national, or global basis? What community or constituency do we serve or represent?

✔ What are our organization's values—the principles that drive our staff and board? How can we state our values positively? For instance, instead of saying "discrimination is wrong," might we say "we promote equality?"

✔ What does our organization want to achieve? What different ways can we express this, beyond our printed mission statement?

If you were interviewing the CEO from a fictional food bank called Foodnet in the fictional town of Springfield, your notes might look something like this:

Foodnet was started by a group of volunteers who organized to provide emergency food during Springfield's 1982 flood. They realized hunger and nutrition problems existed in all weather and seasons. They started providing nondisaster services in 1983.

The need addressed by Foodnet: Hunger and "food insecurity." Some people need food right now to survive. Others need help getting access to food-related services, like food stamps. Others need to improve their budgeting and nutritional skills to improve their use of the resources they have.

We serve two groups: (1) anyone in Springfield County who needs temporary or long-term assistance providing high-quality nutrition to themselves or their families and (2) our volunteers who want to learn about nutrition issues and participate in local solutions.

Values: Food is a right, not a privilege or a luxury. We treat people with respect and help them help themselves. We provide our services with integrity, quality, and cost-effective management.

What we want to achieve: To end hunger in Springfield. To raise community awareness of hunger and nutrition problems. To get the community engaged in solutions. To improve the health of families by empowering them—with knowledge, resources, and skills.

What to Find Out

As you listen and take notes, you may wonder if you are getting bogged down in unnecessary detail. To manage this remember that your goal in this conversation and in Step 1 of the grant-seeking cycle is to learn enough about your organization to communicate accurately and persuasively to others, but no more. Persuasive communication usually does include some details, for example, the anecdote we gave about Orlo's founding; details paint a picture that helps others comprehend both facts and feelings. However, excessively detailed communication can be confusing and obscure the main point.

As you gain experience grant seeking, you will develop the habit of targeting the questions you ask colleagues to get the exact kind of information you need to meet grant requirements, but no more. Grant seeking involves dealing with so much information and so many possibilities that you will always try to target your work in areas that are most likely to get results.

Direction

Your organization has a specific way of responding to the community need you've identified, and funders will want to know about it. They want to know the direction your organization is taking, from your past accomplishments to exactly how you respond with specific programs today, to your vision for tomorrow.

The way this information might be requested by funders varies. A funder may request a "brief statement of history, goals, and accomplishments to date."[5] Or the funder may want more information and say, "Please describe your organization; its mission; its services to youth, including a full description of its innovative components . . . its accomplishments; and its plans."[6] In addition, there may be an explicit or implicit request that you substantiate the appropriateness of your proposed program, given your mission or your capability to carry out a project. In these cases it will be important to highlight your experience and accomplishments.

To prepare for writing these parts of grant proposals, we suggest you ask your CEO the following:

✔ How does our organization go about achieving our purpose? What are our major programs or projects? How do each of these programs contribute toward fulfilling our purpose?

✔ What are the top five accomplishments or milestones that best represent our history and growth? What are you most proud of that we've accomplished recently?

✔ Is there a timeline or written history of our organization?

✔ What about the future? Are we operating from a strategic plan, vision statement, or other overall plan? If so, how was it developed and by whom? May I have a copy of any written vision or plan?

If you were interviewing the CEO from our fictional food bank called Foodnet, your notes might look something like this:

Our programs:

1. The Family Food Resource Center is a place where people can get free emergency food in a respectful and educational setting. Clients "shop" for food just like in a grocery store, learn about nutrition, and find out about Foodnet's other services.

2. The volunteer program provides 90 percent of the labor for all our programs; this engages the community directly in the problems and the solutions.

3. Life Skills classes (at the Food Resource Center) teach food safety, budgeting, and cooking skills to parents of at-risk children.

4. A newly planned program, Rural Food Outreach, will extend our mission to people who can't otherwise access our resource center.

Milestones: 1982—informal group brought food to 682 people isolated by flood. 1983—Foodnet was incorporated; 568 emergency food packages were distributed. 1984—Life Skills education program was introduced.

Future: The board set four organizational goals a year ago and will revisit them this year. There is no complete strategic plan, but the board wants to make one.

Leadership

Potential funders are interested in your ability to carry out a successful program with their money. An important part of this ability is your organization's leadership, and funders will ask about it in one way or another.

Almost all applications will require you to attach a list of your board members with their affiliations, such as where they work. A funder may also ask you to elaborate on your board's qualifications or the qualifications of key paid staff and volunteers outside the board. The way this is phrased on grant application forms could be as basic as a request for "number of board members, full-time paid staff, part-time paid staff and volunteers,"[7] or as frank as "Is the Board strong, knowledgeable and committed to the project?"[8] and "Is there a critical mass of persons for getting the job done?"[9]

The unique missions and interests of funders may be demonstrated in this area. Corporate grant makers may want to know if any of their own employees are involved with your organization (this could make you eligible for additional funding from them in the form of employee-initiated grants or matching donations). A funder with an interest in social justice might want to assess your organization's structure, decision-making base, or commitment to diversity by asking this: "Describe how your organization promotes diversity and addresses inequality, oppression, and discrimination within your organization. Describe any specific steps you are taking to better represent your constituency."[10]

To prepare for writing these parts of grant proposals, you should ask your CEO questions like the following:

✔ Who is our board of directors? How would you describe them as a group? (For example, are they community leaders or experts in their fields?) Is there a printed list with affiliations, such as where board members work, and phone numbers?

✔ Is the board active? How often do they meet? How are board members selected? Is the board of an appropriate size, is it growing, or is recruiting new and active board members currently a critical issue?

✔ How many nonboard volunteers do we have? Generally, what do they do? Do we know where they work, and is that information part of our database? If yes, whom do I ask for that information?

✔ How many paid employees do we have, and what do they do? What are the overall responsibilities of board, staff, and volunteers in comparison to one another?

✔ Are all segments of our constituency reflected in the power sharing and decision making of our organization? For example, if low-income single mothers are the constituency, how many low-income single mothers are on the board and in key volunteer or staff positions?

✔ Does our organization have a demonstrated commitment to diversity, such as a written policy statement, commitments in programs or work plans, public materials, or mission statement? If yes, may I have a copy of any written materials? If no, are we currently making an effort to develop a policy?

✔ Who are the key staff people for whom I should collect resumes or short bios?

If you were interviewing the CEO from our fictional food bank called Foodnet, your notes might look something like this:

The Foodnet board is active and full and meets monthly. Board members are Adrianne X (of Springfield Grocery, former client), Jim A (Bank of Springfield), Carol B (retired, active volunteer), Ani O (attorney), Ella M (Farmers Market organizer, former client). New members are recruited by current board and executive director.

We have more than 50 volunteers working in the food warehouse, as receptionists, on board, and in committees. We have 10 paid employees—executive director, Food Resource Center director, development associate, warehouse manager, emergency director, two Life Skills instructors (seasonally employed by us), 1 part-time bookkeeper, 2 part-time receptionists.

Our board has 5 people, and 2 are former clients who no longer need our services but now contribute as volunteers.

Yes, we have a diversity policy and some existing bios. CEO will give me copies.

Place in the Community

Funders will ask you questions about how your organization fits into and responds to the community. For example, a grant form might say, "Describe the economic characteristics of the area surrounding the location where the funds will be used"[11] or "How long has your organization operated in this community?"[12]

An important part of this concern is how your organization relates to other nonprofits, government agencies, and for-profit organizations. It is very unlikely that your organization is the only one working on your issue, and funders will usually give you the opportunity to show how you are working together with, rather than in opposition to, other parties. For example, one funder writes, "List other groups addressing the same or related objectives and the extent of your coordination with each in developing your proposal."[13]

To prepare for writing these parts of your grant proposals, ask questions like these of your CEO:

✔ How does our organization respond to specific conditions that exist in our neighborhood, town, region, state, or country?

✔ Who else in our community does work similar to ours? How are we similar to these other groups, and how are we different? What makes our organization strategically valuable?

✔ How do we work together with other groups, formally or informally?

✔ Would you say our organization is a leader; if so, how? Are we the largest, first, or most knowledgeable in some area?

If you were interviewing the CEO from our fictional food bank called Foodnet, your notes might look something like this:

> Springfield has a high proportion of people who are not starving but are chronically undernourished. Elderly people on fixed incomes and low-wage agricultural workers have higher health risks because of lack of essential nutrients and over-reliance on certain foods. Foodnet responds with not just food boxes but community involvement and education programs.
>
> We work with: Springfield City government, public schools, and the Springfield Hospital. They all refer clients to us. Springfield Grocery donates food. Springfield College staff help us conduct Life Skills classes.
>
> Similar organizations: the First United Church offers a daily soup kitchen. The Springfield Shelter offers emergency food boxes. We all provide some kind of emergency food for anyone who needs it. We all refer clients to one another— for example, we refer people without cooking facilities to the soup kitchen. But Foodnet is the only one providing longer-term services like nutrition and budgeting education, designed to prevent problems in the future.

Resources

Foundations will scrutinize your use of several kinds of resources: financial, in-kind, volunteer, and physical (such as buildings). They want to know that you have the funds and capacity to carry out a project, that you use the resources you have effectively, and that you have a plan to fund and staff your program in the future without relying on their grants in perpetuity.

The way this concern is phrased on grant application forms will vary. It might be as simple as a request to describe "financial resources available and needed"[14] or, more pointedly, to list "current corporate and foundation funding sources, public and/or private, with amounts contributed within the most recent twelve months."[15] You might also be asked whether you own your facilities or what percentage of your board members are donors.

The values and policies of some funders might be demonstrated here. For example, a funder that gives large donations to the United Way may have a policy against funding United Way agencies individually and so may ask you whether you are one and what "percent of [your] total budget . . . comes from United Way funding."[16]

To formulate complete and convincing answers to these parts of grant proposals, you will need access to budgets, financial reports, donor information, and information about nonfinancial resources (such as volunteers). You will likely need to work with a variety of people to collect this information. For now start with a few questions to your CEO:

✔ What is our organization's total annual budget? Who are our top ten funding sources? Whom can I ask to run a list of these from our records?

✔ Are we a United Way agency?

✔ What is our breakdown of expenses? How much do we spend on administration? Programs? Other major categories appropriate to our organization?

✔ Whom do I ask for copies of individual budgets for each program and for the overall organization's financial statement?

✔ When was the most recent audit completed, and where do I get a copy?

✔ What nonfinancial resources do we have that are critical to our mission? For example, a specially designed or located building, an incredible volunteer base, a strong board of directors, or a crucial partnership with another organization?

✔ What is our current capacity to help our community? Are we able to serve, assist, inform, or include everyone who approaches us, or do we need to turn anyone away for lack of capacity or for any other reason? Are there people we'd like to be including but cannot reach out to? For what reason? What are our limits and limiting factors?

If you were interviewing the CEO from our fictional food bank called Foodnet, your notes might look something like this:

Income: $900,000 total (10% from grants, 30% government contracts, 5% business donations, 5% events, 50% individual donations).

Expenses: $900,000 total (10% administration, 50% Food Resource Center program, 5% Life Skills program, 15% other programs, 10% development, 5% volunteers, 5% buildings and maintenance).

Our warehouse and "shopping" space are our biggest assets, but their size and location limit us to 600 emergency food clients per month. Teaching budget is small, limiting Life Skills classes to 16 per year (about 320 students). The Springfield location of the Food Resource Center limits who can get to us.

We'd like to reach out to rural families in need who don't have transportation to get to us. We have a donated vehicle that we can use to do so.

Impact in the Community

Finally, you will want to know what difference your organization is making in your community. Foundations may not come out and ask this question directly on an organizationwide basis (they will more likely ask you about the impact of a specific program or project you are proposing), but you will want to work this information into your proposals to show that all the research, planning, and hard work carried out by your organization is crucial to your community.

To prepare for writing this message into your proposals, ask your CEO this question:

✔ How would the world (or the city, county, state) be different *without* our organization? How would it be different in a concrete way and in an intangible way?

If you were interviewing the CEO from our fictional food bank called Foodnet, your notes might look something like this:

Without Foodnet, the Springfield population would be less educated about food choices; there would be more hungry people, and less hope.

NEXT STEPS

After your interview with the CEO is over, do this:

→ Save your notes in the folder you created for your organizational resume. You'll come back to these notes in Chapter Five.

If you and your CEO had an easy time coming up with clear answers to these questions, congratulations! You're in good shape to start looking for grants because your answers are exactly the same kind of information funders ask for in proposals. However, if you struggled to answer most of the questions, your organization is probably not ready to move forward on grants. It may be appropriate for you to redirect your labor toward developing the organization until it can provide a clear picture of its identity.

If you're somewhere in the middle, proceed cautiously. In your role as grant seeker you can't solve an organizational identity crisis, but you can use your perception and writing ability to crystallize the things that make your organization unique.

YOUR FIRST-PRIORITY PROGRAM

You might recall from Chapter One that foundation grants tend to pay for specific projects or programs and not for "ongoing normal operations"[17] or "core funding or general operating expenses,"[18] to use the kind of language found in actual grant application forms. Certainly there are exceptions to this generalization. However, if you run the kind of steady, systematic grant-seeking effort we advocate, you'll find that these exceptions are few and far between. Before you start grant seeking, you need to know your organization's individual programs well.

That means you need to conduct another interview, this time focused on the particular identity of a single program or project. This could be a new, planned program, a successful program that is expanding significantly or adding new components, or a physical project like a new computer lab. In light of what you know about your organization and grant seeking so far, do the following:

→ Select just one of your organization's programs or projects to be your first priority for grant seeking, and write it in here:

 _____

Make this choice thoughtfully (and with the approval of your CEO), because for the rest of this book, we'll concentrate on this program. When you've finished the book and set up your grant-seeking system, you can come back and repeat the process for any other program or project you want to fund with grants. (By then it will seem like second nature, and you will progress very quickly.) Here's what to do next:

→ Schedule an appointment with the program director of your highest-priority program. You will need one or two hours of his or her time. Write the date and time of your appointment in here:

 _____

When this appointment time comes, your goal is to get the answers to or learn how to get answers to another set of questions, this time about the program: what it does, whom it involves, and what difference it makes to individuals and the community. Although the questions are described in detail here, you can also find them listed in Exhibit A.2 (in Resource A). Take a copy of this list to your interview, and use it to guide your conversation.

Program directors are deeply involved with the operations of their programs; as you talk with them, you will probably get another workout in the practice of targeting your questions to get the level of detail that funders will be interested in, and no more. For example, you will want to know how many children were served lunch at the day camp, but you don't need to know what they ate for dessert. As you take notes, begin to consider what wording and details might provide the most accurate and persuasive picture of the program.

Name and Purpose

Foundations will ask you to define your project and its purpose in a succinct and compelling way. Although the exact language they use varies, it is usually fairly direct. An example would be, "Describe your project and how it fits into the mission and goals of your organization."[19] You should be able to answer this quickly in a few sentences or less. However, remember that their first impression of your program is often your program's name, written on an application cover sheet or in a cover letter. The name should be short, descriptive, and engaging.

To prepare for writing these parts of grant proposals, ask your program director the same things funders ask for:

✔ What is the name of our program or project?

✔ What is the program's mission? How does it fit within our overall organization's mission and make sense given our values and other programs?

If you were interviewing a program director from our fictional food bank called Foodnet, your notes might look something like this:

Project Name: Rural Food Outreach

Rural Food Outreach will travel out from Springfield to bring Foodnet's successful "shopping"-style food bank to people who are not able to get to Foodnet's downtown Resource Center. The "shopping" model, where people choose their own food, preserves peoples' dignity and self-determination.

This new program shares all the values and some of the methods of our existing programs. It expands our reach and delivers our mission to more people.

The Need the Program Addresses

Funders want to know their donations are meeting a real need that is important in the community. Many foundations tightly focus their giving to one field of service where they know of an existing need. Others that give to a range of causes will likely have staff members or volunteers who are experts in each field in which they make grants. Either way they likely already know about the community need you address, but they will want to read your definition of it.

As you talk with your program director, keep in mind that there may be a difference between the community need your organization as a whole addresses and the need your specific program addresses. For example, we once worked with an organization that generally addressed the needs of low-income people and had many programs. Although their food bank program addressed the issue of hunger, their free health clinic met a specific need for health care for the uninsured.

The way funders ask about this subject will often require you to substantiate the magnitude or significance of the need your program addresses. For example, a funder might ask, "What is the need for your request in terms of both your financial situation and as a community service need? How was the need determined?"[20] or "How important to society is the problem [you address]? Is it of local or wider scope?"[21] Although in Chapter Six we'll go over the job of substantiating the need in more detail, you can start working on it in this interview. Ask your program director questions like these:

✔ Is this program new or ongoing?

✔ If this program is ongoing, why and when was it started? Is it expanding? If so, why?

✔ If the program is new, why is it being created? What is the specific community need for this program?

✔ Can you tell me the story of a person who needs this program?

✔ Do you know of any good sources for statistics to substantiate the need for this program? Would you give me copies of any reports or links to any Web sites you use?

If you were interviewing a program director from our fictional food bank called Foodnet about its fictional new program called Rural Food Outreach, your notes might look something like this:

> This new program is being created because of a need that our board identified for our mission to move outside the city limits and reach more people.
>
> 40% of the Springfield area's population lives outside the city limits and works in agriculture or forestry. They have seasonal food difficulties. Of that rural 40%, at least one-quarter are faced with year-round food insecurity. Many cannot access food box and government programs, which are all located in town, due to limited transportation resources.
>
> One example is the Doe family. They came to work in the Springfield area on a farm, then Dad got hurt on the job. The family is working to stay afloat, but when they need to make rent payments and medical payments, food is the first thing to go. When things get really bad, the Mom gives her food to the youngest kids and doesn't eat for days at a time. Ella, our board member, found out she was doing this and started giving her food at the farmer's market when times were tough. They got to talking about a program that would reach other rural families.

Nuts and Bolts

Funders want basic facts about your program, chiefly who and how many it will serve or involve, its specific methods and activities, and its timeline. The way they phrase this (and the room they give you to answer) will vary tremendously. For example, one foundation might simply ask for "project activities, operational procedures and time schedules,"[22] whereas another could ask eight insightful questions about your "plan" alone, including this: "Is it carefully thought-out and organized?"[23] and "Has a way around possible obstacles been foreseen?"[24] Most hover somewhere in between as far as detail goes, asking you, for example, to "describe the purpose and duration of the program for which you are seeking funds"[25] or requesting that you describe "specific activities for which you seek funding, . . . who will carry out those activities, [and the] time frame in which this will take place."[26]

The timeframe of the project relates to its appropriateness for grant seeking. It is very rare for a funder to make a grant for a project that is completed or substantially under way before their grant decision is made. So in order to give time for grant decisions to be made, your grant requests should go out six to twelve months before your program's starting date. You'll also need to know if there are any formal partnerships with other organizations that are an integral part of the program or that could potentially hold the program back if they're necessary but not yet in place.

To prepare for this part of writing grant proposals, ask your program director questions like these:

- ✔ If our program is new, is this a pilot phase? Of how long?
- ✔ If it is a one-time special project or event, what is its duration, including planning and post-event evaluation?
- ✔ If it is an ongoing program, what is the timeline for expansion?
- ✔ How does the program work? What are the specific services or goods the program will provide to the people it serves?
- ✔ How many people do we plan to serve or involve per year (or total, for one-time events)? What do these people have in common with one another?
- ✔ Are these people involved in the decision making and shaping of the program? If so, how?
- ✔ How long have you been planning this program?
- ✔ Do you have a specific work plan and timeline, and may I have copies of any printed plans?
- ✔ Is this program going to be produced solely by our organization or in partnership or collaboration with other organizations?

✔ If this is a collaboration, is the partnership formal, and do we have a letter of agreement? Or is it informal, in that our organizations rely on one another and enhance each other's work but don't have an official agreement?

If you were interviewing a program director from our fictional food bank called Foodnet about its fictional new program called Rural Food Outreach, your notes might look something like this:

The first year of Rural Food Outreach will be a test phase.

The program serves people and families who all live in the rural outskirts of Springfield and who have limited incomes and food resources. We plan to serve 100 people in the first year.

The program was designed by our board member, Ella, a former client of Foodnet who is now a Farmers Market organizer and the rural family described already.

Our services do the following:

1. The program will deliver monthly supplemental food through visits by our food van—a converted RV which carries food supplies, sort of like a bookmobile for food.
2. Trained outreach volunteers will provide educational materials on food safety and budgeting.
3. The program will provide an interesting and challenging volunteer opportunity for the people of Springfield.

Timeline: First 3 months, planning and stocking van, recruiting from among current volunteers. By 6 months, identify and begin to serve 30 people with monthly van visits, during which they can choose their own food. By the end of the first year, 100 people will be served on a monthly basis.

Rural Food Outreach will be implemented by Foodnet, with the cooperation and referrals of other organizations and with a wide range of community supporters, but no formal partners.

Goals and Vision

Funders want to know that you have some realistic perspective about the project you are proposing. Visions of solving problems are wonderful, but how much will you be able to accomplish in the real world with the limited sum of money you would receive as a grant? To address this issue do the following:

➜ Work together with your program director to clarify the difference between three potentially confusing aspects of your program: its *goals, objectives,* and *methods.*

These three words are not used consistently in common language, and it is unfortunate that the confusion sometimes extends to funders' guidelines. We sort the words out this way:

Goals are the long-term outcomes of the project and may include intangible elements, for example "to increase interracial understanding." A goal for our fictional Rural Food Outreach Program might be "to increase nutrition and access to food choices for rural people."

Objectives are the measurable, shorter-term outcomes, for example, what you could demonstrate to have achieved by the end of the grant period. Objectives can include numbers, such as target dates, service numbers, and survey results. An objective for our fictional Rural Food Outreach program might be "to decrease hunger and food insecurity for 100 people in our first year."

Methods are the means to an end, that is, *how* you will accomplish the objectives and goals. The method for our fictional Rural Food Outreach program might be "by providing monthly food-van outreach, including free food and educational programs, to 100 people in our first year."

No matter which words a funder uses, in order to write clear proposals you need to be able to distinguish *what* your program is trying to accomplish from *how* it tries to accomplish it. Your conversation on this issue may reveal interesting things you can use in your grant proposals, for example, previously unspoken assumptions about the way your program works and research in your program director's field of knowledge.

To put this discussion in perspective, end this part of your interview by asking your program director to dream a bit. Ask this:

✔ What is your vision for the future of this program? If you had all the funding you desired, how would you operate the program? What's your dream in relation to this issue?

If you were interviewing the program director for our fictional Rural Food Outreach program, your notes might read this way:

We envision Rural Food Outreach growing to the point where the van is in operation every weekday, serving a route that visits every rural family in need at least once per month. Our dream is to leave no one hungry.

Resources

Just like your overall organization, each program needs several kinds of resources. When a funder asks you to "describe the resources in place for this program," this kind of open-ended question is your opportunity to describe your great volunteer base, accomplished staff, and donated warehouse, theater space, or van.

However, funders are considering giving you money, so in addition to news of other kinds of resources, this part of your proposal should contain financial information. Although they vary in their aversion to risk, funders don't want to give to a project that will run short of cash and not get carried out or that is likely to fail. Your existing resources (or your ability to solicit all the necessary resources for a project) are important parts of your pitch to a funder.

You'll need to tell each funder the budget for your program, how you plan to spend their grant, and what portion of your total budget you are requesting from them. This may be phrased with language such as "Include a detailed project budget (projected expenditures and revenues) including how the major elements are estimated."[27]

Besides the basic expenses of your program, this part of the proposal requires you to be knowledgeable about other donations that have been sought or received. Recall from Chapter One that foundations usually do not want to be the sole funder of a project and that they probably do not want to be approached to fund it again once it is established and ongoing. These concerns about current and future funding may be merely implicit, such as guidelines that ask you to "describe other possible sources of support which have been or will be solicited for the project, including a statement of funds which have been received or pledged."[28] Or they might be stated baldly, for example in guidelines that ask, "If [your] project is successful, how will it be funded in the future?"[29]

To prepare for writing this part of your grant proposals, you'll want to ask your program director questions like these:

✔ What is the estimated cost for this project? If it is a multiple-year project, such as a three-year pilot phase or expansion phase, what is the total cost as well as each year's cost?

✔ May I have copies of any written budgets and any quotes from vendors or other documentation of how costs were arrived at?

✔ If the program is new, what specific things are needed to get it started?

✔ If the program is ongoing, what specific things are needed to keep going or to expand? Why seek a grant at this particular time?

✔ What resources are already in place for this project? Other grants or funding sources (and their amounts)? Donations? Physical resources, such as a space or vehicles? Volunteers?

✔ What other funding is being sought? Have proposals already been sent to any other potential funders? Are there reasons why particular funders might be interested?

✔ If the program is meant to continue in the future, how will it be funded after an initial grant or grants? Thinking creatively, how can we go beyond "looking for more grants"? For example, will the program cost less annually after it is established? Will it generate any of its own money through earned income? Is it especially appropriate for in-kind donations? Will it build philanthropy among a particular group of people who may give to it in the future?

✔ Who are the key personnel (paid or unpaid), and what are their qualifications? Do you have any written bios or resumes for them, or how can I reach them to ask about their qualifications? What portion of each person's time is going to be dedicated to this program or project?

If you were interviewing a program director from our fictional food bank program called Rural Food Outreach, your notes might look something like this:

We estimate Rural Food Outreach will cost $52,000 in its first year.

Ella (board member) has experience as a former Foodnet client and in her work with farmers through the local Farmers Market. Susan has been the executive director of Foodnet for ten years and developed our successful Food Resource Center. She has a degree in public health from Springfield University; 25% of her time will be dedicated to establishing this program.

We already have an RV that is converted for a similar use. It was donated to us by the Springfield Service Club who used it for vision screenings. We have received $1,000 from the Farmers Market of Springfield volunteer committee.

In particular, the Springfield Dairy might be interested in funding the program because it serves the region directly surrounding their plant.

Specific needs include funding for a staff person to oversee the program, food to stock the van, printed educational materials, gas, and insurance.

Families participating in Rural Food Outreach are sometimes farmers, and our hope is that they will eventually be able to contribute a few in-kind goods to the van in return for the "shopping" they do. This will help redistribute fresh food among all the people who use the program. In addition, we will create a donor program, where donors join for $100 per year to be a Rural Food Outreach supporter.

Evaluation and Impact

Funders want to know that their grants are successful and that they are given to programs whose leaders are effective and somewhat objective in their administration. In the past decade there has been a growing expectation that grantees will provide hard data on program evaluation. Most funders will ask you about your plans to evaluate your program or project, and they will want your plans to be appropriate for your project's scope and focus.

For example, you wouldn't want to propose a paid third-party evaluation in a proposal for a $2,000 grant to buy a new copy machine. However, in an $800,000 grant proposal for expanding a successful statewide program over several years, a rigorous longitudinal study by professional researchers might be in order. For an ongoing program that is expanding or changing, funders will want to know why this particular program should grow and may base your potential future success on your track record.

Although evaluation is a crucial element of grant proposals, in most cases funders don't expect a research-journal-quality scientific analysis or want you to spend a majority of your funds and time on evaluation. They do want to know that you have a way to assess the effectiveness of your own work and its impact on peoples' lives, as well as a guide by which to make adjustments to your program when needed. The way funders ask for this information can vary. Usually it will be something like "describe how the project's effectiveness will be determined."[30] Words like *outcome* and *impact* may also be used.

Requests like this clue you in that this section of the grant proposal may be an opportunity to discuss not just the immediate effects of your program but the ripple effect your program will have in your community, that is, on people and issues beyond those directly served. For example, you might argue that decreasing school dropouts could reduce early pregnancy, thus affecting educators, health care providers, and future generations of children.

To prepare for writing this part of your grant proposals, ask your program director questions like these:

✔ How will our program be evaluated? Who will evaluate it and how often? What exactly will be measured to determine success?

✔ If the program is ongoing, has this evaluation been done before? What were the results?

✔ What will be done with future evaluation results? For example, will the program change as a result of evaluation feedback?

✔ In addition to the people who are directly served or involved, who else will our program affect? Think about this list of possible groups or people that the program will have an effect on: direct participants, their families, their children, neighbors, specific populations, schools, law enforcement, health care providers, faith centers or churches, service clubs, local businesses, government, other nonprofit organizations, other groups that are particular to our program or the whole community.

✔ Do you have letters of support from any of these groups, or could you identify two or three we can call to request letters?

If you were interviewing the program director from our fictional food bank program called Rural Food Outreach, your notes might look something like this:

Rural Food Outreach will be evaluated at six and twelve months by a team consisting of the program's director, our executive director, and one board member. Evaluation will consist of interviews with participating families and statistics collected about how many people use the service and what food they receive. The program director will use the evaluation to determine if changes are needed to the program.

Rural Food Outreach benefits direct participants with food and education. It helps participants' children by giving their parents the tools to provide nutritional meals for them.

Ripple effect: The program will benefit health care providers by creating new access to nutritious food. It will extend the work of churches, service clubs, and other nonprofits who provide emergency food in town and will provide them with a volunteer opportunity. It will benefit the local government by creating a solution to a difficult problem, and it will benefit the whole community with its spirit of volunteerism and education.

We have a letter of support from First United Church and could get one from Springfield Elementary school's nutritionist. Ella will call her.

Extra Questions for Certain Projects

The questions you've asked your program director in this chapter pertain primarily to direct-service programs and projects such as soup kitchens, educational programs, and art exhibits and performances. Although most of the same information is needed for capital and capacity-building grant proposals, these are special kinds of applications that deserve their own targeted questions, for example, information on your building site or a five-year development plan. You may need the advice of a professional development consultant or a book focused on the area in which you're working to complement this one.

NEXT STEPS

After your interview with the program director is over, do this:

→ Save your notes in the folder you created for your first-priority program (in our example, the folder "Rural Food Outreach").

Then take a well-deserved break as you let this material settle in your mind. Answering these questions has in all likelihood challenged your organization and is probably the most laborious work in this book. Now that you have answered them, you have prepared yourself to write not just one grant proposal but dozens.

Synthesize What You've Learned So Far

In this chapter we'll take a break from gathering information about your organization so you can start working with what you already have. We'll start off easy, composing some of the standard documents that will nearly always be attached to your grant proposals, for example, your list of board members. Then we'll challenge you to summarize what you've learned about your organization and first-priority program into short "resumes." By the end of the chapter your files will be filled with material you can use in your future grants, and you'll have gone through a workout designed to leave you toned up for the task of writing proposal text.

GATHERING BASE MATERIALS

Grant proposals are usually packages with several parts. After a cover sheet, there is a main narrative—perhaps a lengthy application form to fill out or a set of questions to answer. And then there are a number of attachments, mostly standard documents about your organization that are regularly required in grant proposals, for example, your 501(c)(3) letter from the IRS. Although it's easy to concentrate on the narrative, the grant proposal really is a complete package, and you should take care with all of its parts, making sure they all fit together and present a unified theme. So you can get an idea of what we mean, a complete grant proposal is provided in Resource B.

After your recent interviews with your CEO and program director, you should be ready to produce the standard documents we call base materials (to emphasize that they form the base of every strong proposal). As you gather or create these materials, you'll make several copies. That way you are always ready to attach them to a proposal without having to stop at the copy machine repeatedly.

→ To begin, acquire the following documents relating to your organization:

- *501(c)(3) letter:* the letter from the IRS confirming that your organization is a tax-exempt charity
- *Most recent form 990:* the "tax return" most nonprofits file with the IRS
- *Bylaws:* the internal "constitution" of your organization, describing board powers and other basic legal matters
- *Letters of support* and *newspaper clippings* about your organization
- *Organizational budget for the current year:* the projected budget for your whole organization (not detailed program budgets)
- *Current financial statement:* a document comparing your projected organizational budget to current actual income and expenses (you'll need to get this periodically from your bookkeeper or accountant)
- *Last two audited financial statements:* documents created by an independent auditor that include assets, liabilities, and other items they deem appropriate (from your bookkeeper or accountant)

These base materials can often be photocopied unaltered and dropped into grant proposals. In fact, changing an IRS letter or official audit would invalidate it. Therefore you should do this:

→ Make ten copies of each document.
→ Put the copies in file folders designated for them in your Organizational and Program files, which you created in Chapter Three.

CHOOSING A LOOK

There are other base materials you will need, and these you can exercise more control over. They may take a little more work on your part, but you can use the opportunity to help build a consistent look for your grant materials, adding to your proposal presentation and eliminating future worries about how to format your work.

→ Locate the following documents about your organization, or create rough drafts of them in your word processing program, but don't copy or file them yet:

- *List of board members:* Include names, business affiliations, addresses, and phone numbers (information required by many funders).
- *Bios of key people:* Three or four sentences should be sufficient for each person, including the CEO, board president and directors, and *key* volunteers of the programs that are high priorities for grants. (If you are working on a capital campaign or capacity-building grant, you will also want your development director's bio.)
- *Antidiscrimination policy:* This is an official statement your organization may have describing its policies against discrimination in the workplace and in its services (sometimes required by a funder).

Now evaluate these documents in light of the fact that they will likely be incorporated into grant proposals. Think about what it would be like to work for a funder and review these documents after reading a five- to ten-page narrative. Are these documents easily readable? Do they generally match each other in font and format? Is the type big enough or too tiny? Are they messy or dirty from repeated copying, or are they printed on overly expensive or fancy paper?

This is a good time for you to create a simple and clean look you can use for all your base materials and many of your future grant proposals. Your goal is to look focused and organized without appearing flashy or wasteful. Someone who can pay for impressive color printing may not seem to need a $5,000 grant. However, someone whose materials are printed on the backs of recycled memos may come across as too informal. You want to send the message that you are capable, you need funding, and your organization will be a good steward of any money you receive.

The font you use should be easy to read. Remember that funders read a lot, and you don't want to make their job any harder. We suggest a common font like Times New Roman in a relatively large size such as 12 or 12.5 point. When you use formatting like bold, italics, and so on, keep their use consistent. For example, if titles are centered and underlined on one piece, they should be that way on all pieces.

Although you might like to save paper, consider the fact that foundation staff often drop your proposal into a big copy machine, and you don't want them to miss anything. We recommend printing your base materials and all proposal materials on only one side of the page. Exceptions are your IRS letter, audits, and any long financial statements; these can be two-sided unless you're directed otherwise by the funder. Be careful with illustrations and shades of gray; they may not copy clearly. Once you have considered these issues, do this:

→ Create or refashion your board list, key biographies, and antidiscrimination policy on your word processor, creating a consistent and easily readable look as you go.

→ Save these documents in the "Organization and Program" folder on your computer, and file ten copies of each paper document in the appropriate files in your file cabinet.

Now you are the proud owner of several items that will speed the creation of your next ten grant proposals. You have most of the attachments you'll need, as well as a house style that will guide the formatting for the rest of your work. You can cross a few worry-inducing variables off your mental list.

CREATING ORGANIZATIONAL AND PROGRAM RESUMES

When we first began grant seeking in a small town in Oregon, we traveled to the big city of Portland for a panel presentation, where a program officer from a major Oregon foundation was speaking. She noted that her job, which consisted partly of summarizing applicants' information for her trustees, would be easier and more foolproof if applicants would do that summarizing for her. She asked that we make an effort to present our entire organization on one page.

It didn't sound easy, but we realized if we could make a program officer's work life easier, it might make our message more understandable and effective. So we came up with the *organizational resume*—a single sheet that can stand on its own and has all the basic facts that foundations typically request. Researching and creating it is one of the first steps we take when grant seeking for any organization. An example is shown in Exhibit 5.1.

Note how the resume includes all the basic facts regularly requested in grant proposals, such as

- Your organization's name, address, phone, fax, e-mail, and Web address
- Your organization's mission
- A list or short description of your programs or services
- Your geographic service area
- The founding date and timeline of key points in your history
- The name of your CEO, with phone number
- The name of your board president, with phone number
- Your total annual budget
- Where your money comes from (best expressed in percentages)
- Where it goes (best expressed in percentages)
- How many paid staff and how many volunteers you employ

Now it's time for you to take a crack at your own organizational resume. To start:

→ Get out your notes from the interview you conducted with your CEO, and have your organizational files close at hand. These are your raw ingredients.

→ Select, summarize, and edit until you've constructed a one-page summary of your organization like the one shown in Exhibit 5.1.

It will be challenging to get your information on one page, but consider it practice in the useful habit of *limiting* information to what's crucial and relevant and in writing clearly and concisely. Try to imagine the kind of information people from outside your organization would want. What kind of statements will help them understand your group and get a clear picture of its value? What kind of details will just confuse them?

Although you should stick generally to your house style, this kind of resume is one of the few places it is okay to reduce your margins and type size. But remember, this isn't just an exercise. This document will be used, so make sure it

Exhibit 5.1. Organizational Resume

Dragon's Breath International

A nonprofit organization dedicated to promoting fun, friendship, and fitness, primarily through teaching and competing in the traditional Chinese sport of dragon boating.

Contacts

Board President, Rob Thompson, 503.222.2222   444 West X Street, Portland, Oregon 970XX
Head Coach, Stephanie Dyck, 503.222.2222   www.battan.com/dbi/

History

1989	The Portland-Kaohsiung Sister City Association chose dragon boat racing as an annual cultural event to be held in Portland, Oregon.
1992	Dragon's Breath International (DBI) was founded by a group of friends who wanted to participate as a team, paddling the 40-foot long colorful dragon-shaped boats.
1998	DBI was one of 2 teams to represent the U.S. in the World Club Crew Championships in New Zealand.
1998	We added a novice team and grew to 50 paddlers; our novice team earned the silver medal in its division at the largest dragon boat festival in the U.S.
1999	DBI won the gold medal, Recreational Division, at the Vancouver Lake Regatta.
2000	Top U.S. team in the Recreational Division, at the Vancouver, British Columbia, Dragon Boat festival

Current programs

- Today DBI is one of the top competitive dragon boat racing teams in Portland and the Pacific Northwest.
- We have taught more than 100 Portlanders to paddle dragon boats competitively and supported them in making fitness an integral and enjoyable part of their lives.
- We maintain our competitive position in an atmosphere of good will toward other teams, toward our community, and toward visitors to our city who find our sport fascinating.
- Each year, we complete a volunteer project, pulling together other teams with whom we normally compete.

Resources

Number of paid staff:	0
Number of volunteers:	30–40
Number of board members:	5
Board meets:	6 times annually
DBI's total annual budget:	$35,890

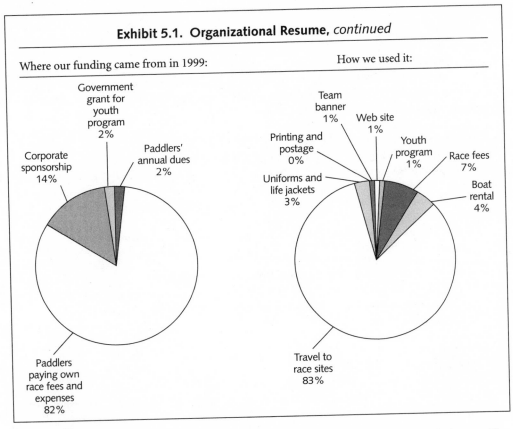

Exhibit 5.1. Organizational Resume, *continued*

Where our funding came from in 1999:

Government grant for youth program 2%

Paddlers' annual dues 2%

Corporate sponsorship 14%

Paddlers paying own race fees and expenses 82%

How we used it:

Team banner 1%

Web site 1%

Printing and postage 0%

Youth program 1%

Race fees 7%

Uniforms and life jackets 3%

Boat rental 4%

Travel to race sites 83%

is readable. You can attach it to your final grant proposals to give foundation staff a useful snapshot of your organization. Giving them summarized information may ease their workload and ensure that your story is told accurately to their trustees.

Once you've finished preparing this resume, do this:

→ Run it by your CEO for approval before finalizing it.

→ Make ten copies of the final version, and file them in your "Organizational Resume" folder.

→ Congratulate yourself, because you're farther along toward finishing your first proposal than you might imagine.

Because grant proposals are usually about specific programs and projects, it's also a good idea to make a resume for each program for which you are seeking grant funding. To see an example of a program resume, see Exhibit 5.2.

Exhibit 5.2. Program Resume

Port City Partnership for the Arts

PCPA was founded in 1992, to help our member arts organizations reach broader audiences and build a sustainable, networked cultural community in Port City. We now have 32 member organizations, with a wide variety of missions and sizes.

Art Patrons for the 21st Century ("Project 21C")

Project 21C will develop the next generation of arts-goers and patrons in Port City, by engaging young people new to arts attendance in a low-cost year-long program of education, events, performances, and social interaction. Project 21C will serve people with little experience attending our city's museums, galleries, ballet, symphony, theatre performances, and film festivals.

Our goal is to create new interest in the arts among a young and vital segment of our population. We project that by the end of the first operating year:

- 750 first-time or infrequent arts-goers will have joined the program.
- More than 400 will have attended at least six arts events and received 6 educational pieces.
- Long-term evaluation will show that participants have increased their arts attendance after the program period is over.

Our resources
- First-year cost: $275,000
- Already committed: $125,000 from the A Foundation and the B Foundation
- Volunteers: 12 local artists and young community leaders will form a Leadership Team
- Each partner agency has agreed to assist PCPA in raising $10,000 toward the project.

Our partners

Port City Art Museum, Far Flung Gallery, The Ballet Company, Port City Symphony, Port Area Rep, Salamander Theatre, Port Shakespeare Co., The Film Institute, Port University, and Port City Parks

Our case

A vital and active arts community is crucial to any healthy city. Young people must feel welcomed and engaged by the arts in order to participate fully, so that we may all be better educated and more inspired by the work of our city's artists.

PCPA—a unique organization that brings together nonprofit arts entities who would typically be competing rather than working together—is the one and only organization with the experience, mission, and existing partnerships to successfully carry out this program.

Our contact information

Port City Partnership for the Arts Executive Director, Jorge Klein, 999.222.2222
Project 21C Coordinator, Oni Schuman, 999.222.2222
www.webaddressforportcitypartnership.xx

Like the organizational resume, the program resume anticipates information that funders will need and want to know. It should be able to stand on its own, so it will briefly repeat some of the information that is on your organizational resume. It should include things like these:

- Your organization's name and briefly stated mission
- Your program or project name
- The program's "mini-mission" and how it fits within your whole organization's mission
- The geographic area covered, if relevant
- Who will be served or who will participate (number and description)
- The timeline of when this program (or expansion of a program) will happen
- A bulleted list of measurable objectives
- Contact information, including phone number, for the program's director or key volunteer (someone who can answer questions)
- Contact information for your CEO
- Resources needed, as well as those you have in place for this project
- Who will benefit
- Why you are the right organization to operate this program or project
- Any formal partners in the program, such as other nonprofits that are working in a coalition with yours

There is no substitute for practice, so do this:

→ Review your notes from your interview with the program director from your first-priority program.
→ Write up a one-page resume for your first-priority program like the one in Exhibit 5.2.

Once again it may seem impossible to get the program resume on one page, but it can be done and will be appreciated by foundation staff. Just focus on what's essential and what outsiders need to know to understand the program and its value. When it comes time to write out a full proposal, you'll often have room there for a fuller and more expressive narrative.

When you are satisfied with your program resume, do this:

→ Run it by your CEO and relevant program director for approval.

→ Make ten copies of it, and file it in the folder for the program it describes.

CONGRATULATIONS

Writing these resumes is probably the hardest job in the entire book. If you've survived them without cheating, give yourself a pat on the back and a few hours off before heading into the next chapter.

Learn About Your Community

When a member of a funder's staff sits down to read a proposal you've written, she looks for a strong connection between the money her organization can give, the project you want to do, and an authentic need for that project. When she looks for that need, she will usually be thinking of the community's needs, not your organization's needs. Your community youth center might truly require a new roof, but the kind of need the funder will probably want to hear about first is the number of neighborhood children with nowhere to go after school.

Substantiating the community need is more than just a necessity in a grant proposal. Because the funders you apply to often have some knowledge about the field you work in, this part of your proposal can be a test of your organization's competence and knowledge. This section of the grant can show you've done your homework and you understand your field. Even though you already know something about your community's need from your interviews with your CEO and program director, it's also necessary to do some independent research.

HOW TO QUANTIFY THE NEED

You will require some statistics to give credibility to your arguments, but you don't need to spend months with your nose buried in books or Web sites. For social service, arts, and some environmental grants the standard for statistical substantiation of need is not as rigorous as in academia or science. For most proposals under

$100,000, two or three research sources are all you'll need (or will have room) to include; in many cases you'll have less than a page to describe your community's need. If you have more space, it's not necessarily better to use more. A proposal that is heavy on statistics can be drier, harder to read, and less persuasive than one that uses numbers judiciously. Remember that your habits should be to target your efforts and limit information to the essential.

Before you start looking for research sources, take a moment to consider exactly what kind of information you're seeking. Think for a few minutes about all the different kinds of numbers that might be useful to you. For example, if you are working for a children's literacy program, you might be able to use statistics about children, poverty, literacy, education, and volunteerism. If your program is statewide, you'll want population and school statistics for the whole state, as well as for the counties or towns where your program is expanding.

Anticipate making a broad survey of different kinds of information before getting into too much detail. You want to see what's out there, then zero in and get more detail from the two or three sources that are most relevant and evocative. For example, for the literacy program described earlier you might want to include state education department statistics about school drop-out rates, but you might also find that a certain percentage of low-income children have no books in their homes. The first might be a highly relevant statistic; the second evokes a picture of a deserving child.

Go through the following set of questions to get started on your research:

✔ Think about the program for which you're raising funds. What are some key-words that describe the area of need or subject focus?

✔ Read through the notes you took during your conversations with your CEO and program director. Did they give you any leads on statistics regarding the community condition(s) you address?

✔ What is the geographic region you are covering? Which cities, counties, states, and so on?

✔ Do you have any reliable and up-to-date statistics already? Where did your existing material come from? (This might be a good place to start looking for more.)

✔ Who at your organization might know where to get more?

If a grant seeker were to go through this exercise for an imaginary literacy program, her notes might look like this:

Keywords: *literacy, poverty, education*

Existing leads: Amelia, the program director, said Department of Education has stats about school dropouts.

Geographic region: statewide, with a focus on X, Y, and Z counties.

Research in hand: I found some 3-year-old school stats on federal free lunch eligibility in the previous grant writer's files. They're from the Department of Education; I should contact them for more recent stats.

People here who might have more leads: Amelia and Mark (the executive director).

Although you may only use two or three statistical or research sources in each of your grant proposals, it's a good idea to have at least a half dozen in your files when you sit down to write. This isn't necessarily as much work as it sounds. One afternoon split between the library and the office can acquaint you with the sources we describe next.

The Internet

You may want to turn to the Internet first. It's easy to make a broad survey of what's available in your field; you don't need to leave your office, and the Internet contains a wealth of information. Often you can download complete research papers or government reports that could otherwise take weeks to locate and order.

However, you have to be careful about using what you find on-line. Remember that anyone can publish a Web page and say anything on it they like. That may not matter when you're looking for gossip about Star Trek, but for the purpose of writing your grant proposals, you want to find the most credible information possible—for example, from government agencies, research institutes, and other reputable nonprofit organizations.

→ Using Internet search engines, find one new and credible source of statistics on your subject area, and bookmark it on your computer.

Newspapers

Newspapers are a good place to start your paper search for community information. Some make their archives available on-line, but there can be a vast amount of published information that newspapers do not provide on their Web sites and that you will need to find at the library.

Larger regional and national papers often run stories with statistical tables or graphs alongside. For example, a newspaper might run a story about public kindergartens around the state, with a graph of the rates of reading readiness in various counties, just what we need for our literacy program. These kinds of news stories and sidebars can give you statistics directly and clue you in to what agencies and experts are working on the subject. Familiarize yourself with your regional newspaper's Web site and how much information is available through on-line archives. Search for your topic and find one statistic you could use to substantiate the community need for your organization's services. Save the information on your computer in your "Community" folder.

➔ Go to the library (or in some cases your library's Web site), and search for stories on your topic with the full-text newspaper indexes available on computers there. Ask a librarian to get you started if you haven't used these before. Work until you've found at least one more relevant statistic. Print or e-mail yourself this material.

Government Agencies

There are dozens of federal and state agencies that keep statistics on their subject areas and give the results out for free, from the Department of Agriculture to the National Endowment for the Arts. It's often possible to ask the employees who compiled the reports to help you understand the results. You just have to locate the right person.

➔ Using the results of your research so far—or even the government section of your phone book—find one agency that looks relevant. Call and ask general questions like, "I'm studying the subject of literacy and wondered if anyone there keeps statistics about it." If you find a knowledgeable person, write his or her name and number in here:

Librarians

Librarians can help you navigate the reams of information you may find available on the Internet, on library shelves, and in government reports. Don't be shy about asking questions. If you go to a librarian with a clear idea of the questions you want to answer, he may save you weeks of brutal wading through the subject by yourself. If you have access to a university library, you may be able to find a gold mine: a librarian who specializes in your subject.

→ Talk to the librarian about what you're trying to achieve and what you've found so far. Write the librarian's name and suggestions in here:

Academics and Other Experts

In all likelihood someone in a university somewhere has spent most of her life researching exactly the kind of questions you have just a day or two to tackle. If you call prepared and show you know a little about the subject at hand, she will probably be pleased to talk to you and give you the benefit of her expertise. She can help you understand what the numbers in those government reports mean, saving you a lot of frustration and time.

→ Using the results of your research so far or an Internet search, find a professor who has written or taught about your subject area. Call or e-mail that person with some intelligent questions. Write his or her name and e-mail address here:

You ought to have plenty of leads on research material by now. To finish up this part of your work and clear your desk of all the evidence:

→ File the research materials you've collected so far in your Community files, for example, in your "Statistics" and "Press Clippings" folders.

WHY YOU NEED TO COLLECT STORIES

Although statistics will be necessary to substantiate community needs in your proposals, stories about individual people can add interest to dry numbers like poverty rates or theater ticket sales. We strongly suggest you use stories to break up the numbers you are presenting and remind the reader of the real people who will benefit from a grant. Stories are often referred to as anecdotal evidence of a community need; they show the kind of people who are or could be affected by your organization's work.

During your interview with the program director of your first-priority program, you asked for stories. Now that your other research has given you some relevant background information, you may want to review those stories. Decide whether they illustrate a community need and whether they back up or expand on any of the statistics you found on the Internet and at the library.

With your new perspective you'll probably find you want more stories. If so, do this:

→ Call or sit down with one or two program staff from your highest-priority program. During this call or meeting, ask for stories about people who need their program (if it is proposed but not yet operating) or who needed it in the past (if the program is already operating).

Although it's natural to focus on individual success stories, you're currently investigating the community's *need* for your organization's services, not your own program's effectiveness. So focus on stories about how your organization knew that someone needed help. What was life like for that child, adult, or family *before* they participated in your programs?

Pursuing this kind of inquiry often gets staff talking about details that can be important to your understanding of community needs and evocative in your proposal writing. For example, we once worked with a program for homeless youth, where we were handed some printed material that stated community needs. Reading this material, we learned that there were an estimated 1,200 homeless youth in our city and that they had various health and safety problems that were caused by their homelessness.

But when we simply asked what a homeless teenager's life was like, we learned some surprising things: that homeless youth often lead nocturnal lives and have trouble adjusting to normal daytime activities such as school; that their lives seem random, and they lose a sense of cause and effect for their actions; and that they tend to have chronic health problems, such as respiratory illnesses, from being cold.

When we wrote a grant proposal, we used details like these to paint a picture of just one of those teens—a picture that helped the reader perceive the accompanying statistics as more than just numbers. There weren't just 1,200 homeless teens but 1,200 young people in our city living this kind of life. A story about one of them was powerful enough to communicate the urgent needs of the other 1,199. Stories can be so persuasive that you should make collecting them a consistent and ongoing part of your grant-seeking work.

HOW TO RESEARCH OTHER NONPROFITS

There are hundreds of thousands of nonprofits in the United States, and if you are addressing a real need, it is extremely unlikely that you're the only organization working on the issue. Foundation staff will be correctly skeptical of a claim that your organization is the only one doing what you do, and you don't want to give them the impression you're operating in a vacuum.

As a courageous grant seeker you're not afraid of other nonprofits or in denial that they exist and can do a good job. You will want to find out about other organizations, agencies, and people who are working in your community to address the same or similar need your organization addresses. The interviews you conducted with the CEO and program staff give you a good place to start. You may have collected the names of several nonprofit organizations and government agencies with which your organization works.

➔ Using those names or looking on the World Wide Web, in the telephone book, or through a local referral service or call to a librarian, list up to five organizations that have similar missions or programs to yours, preferably in your town or region. Write their names, phone numbers, and Web addresses in here (for example, First Catholic Church, 555–1212, www.fcc.zzz):

 _____

➜ Contact each of the five organizations with a casual phone call or e-mail. Don't grill them; just say you're interested in what they do. Ask them to send you their brochures and put you on their mailing lists.

Getting brochures and other mailings is an easy way to keep up-to-date with other organizations. (With your name on their lists, you will probably receive their fundraising letters as well.) As these materials start to come in, you will be tempted to sit down and read them right away. But as an efficient grant seeker, you need to develop a crucial habit: dividing your time into blocks for different types of work. This habit helps you control and comprehend all the information you are bombarded with and makes your work time more concentrated and effective. So rather than read your mail as it arrives, do this:

➜ Place all your incoming mail in your folder marked "To Read and Consider."
➜ Once a day or once a week, depending on your work schedule, review all your mail at once.
➜ File appropriate materials in the file you marked "Newsletters and Material from Other Nonprofits."

E-mail has become a standard way of communicating, so we suggest developing a similar habit for e-mail, that is, checking and filing it once a day, and once a day only.

WHAT'S NEXT

It may seem like you're more than ready to write a grant proposal at this point. You've made a major investment in learning and probably could sit down right now and write a proposal in under a day. But to whom? In order to write a *great* proposal—one that's targeted to get results—you have one more kind of research to perform before you move to Step Two of the grant cycle. The last part of Step One is learning about funders.

chapter SEVEN

Learn About Funders

Even if you were applying for just one grant, you'd have to find out about the funder, the details of the opportunity, and the application guidelines. Any grant seeker can do that. As an *efficient* grant seeker you do a bit more and reap the rewards. You realize you'll be seeking numerous small and mid-sized grants each year, so you check out a number of prospective funders at one time. You realize that even though grant seeking is a rational process, funders don't always publish formal statements about their giving that reflect exactly what they do. So you research each one to get some idea of how the funder acts. You pick the funders you apply to as carefully as they pick you.

In this chapter we'll take you on a tour of ways to find funders and learn more about them. You'll get to flex your muscles and practice each step, generating at least ten funding leads, then following through to define the ways they match with your organization. As in the last chapter, keep your focus on your top-priority program, but if along the way you see something that would be great for another program, make a note of it. You can come back to it later.

GENERATING NEW LEADS

Although funders you don't know and have never worked with are probably not your best prospects in the short term, it will be difficult to increase your annual grant income without them. There's no substitute for generating new leads and initiating new relationships. Once a month or so (more frequently if your grant seeking is just getting started) you should make a trip to cyberspace and the library to spend a few hours looking for new opportunities. In between those searches you should always be on the lookout. In the sections to follow we walk you through several standard ways of generating new leads and give you practice doing important, related work.

First we need a definition of *lead*. A *lead* is a funder you hear of or find out about by surfing or scanning information sources. By *getting leads* we just mean identifying the names of funders who are working in your organization's general field of interest and obtaining their contact information such as name, address, phone, and Web address. At this stage don't bog yourself down doing detailed research on funders. That kind of research will come soon enough.

Foundation Center Libraries and Cooperating Collections

The Foundation Center is an organization established by foundations to provide a standard source of information on corporate and foundation giving. It maintains several hundred collections of grant-related reference books located in libraries around the United States.

➜ Look up the location and hours of the closest Foundation Center library or cooperating collection. As of this writing you can get this information by calling (800) 424–9836 or by visiting their Web site at www.fdncenter.org. Write the location and hours in here:

 _____

A Trip to the Library

Foundation Center collections are often located within large university or public libraries. In addition, most mid- to large-size public libraries will likely have some reference books to use for funder research. Between the Foundation Center publications and other grant-related material at your library, you can make a single trip a rich source of leads.

➜ Schedule a half-day or day trip to a Foundation Center library or collection or to a large public or university library to work on the sources of leads we describe next.

The Foundation Directory[1] and Related Resources. The Foundation Center maintains a large database of several kinds of grant-related information. As of this writing, the center covers over fifty thousand foundations and corporate donors, with associated files describing hundreds of thousands of grants given and trustee names. Portions of this database are currently published in several formats, including printed books, CD-ROM databases, and pay-for-access Internet databases. You should be able to use most of these publications for free at your local Foundation Center library or collection. Some of these publications will be more helpful to you than others.

The printed *Foundation Directory* has been called the bible of grant sources. Now published in multiple volumes due to the tremendous growth in the number of foundations represented, Part 1 contains listings for the ten thousand biggest foundations, in terms of assets, in the United States. The entry for each funder contains their contact information, trustee names, statements about their purpose and guidelines, and some descriptions of grants given. Part 2 contains the same kind of information for the next ten thousand biggest foundations.

➔ At the library get to know the *Foundation Directory* by looking up one funder relevant to you. This is your first lead. Photocopy the entry or write the funder's name and contact information in here (for example, "XYZ Foundation"):

✍ Contact name: _____

✍ Contact information: _____

➔ When you get back to your office later, you will do what you always do when you get a new lead. Take your lead's contact information and drop it in your "Funders to Contact" folder.

Another printed volume from The Foundation Center is more intriguing to us. *Foundation Grants Index* gives descriptions of about one hundred thousand grants of $10,000 or more that were actually made in a given year. What makes this uniquely useful is that it reflects what grant makers actually fund, which may or may not be exactly the same as their guidelines indicate. You can try to find appropriate leads by looking at who gave grants to organizations in your field or to organizations similar to your own.

→ Use *Foundation Grants Index* to generate one lead relevant to your organization. Photocopy the contact information for the funder you've discovered or write it in here:

✍ Foundation: _____

✍ Contact name: _____

✍ Contact information: _____

Although the *Foundation Directory* and the *Foundation Grants Index* are certainly valuable, most small organizations do not need to purchase these books. Unless you have a special situation or a national program, your first success in systematic grant seeking is likely to come from local sources, with relatively small grants. Because they only include the largest funders and grants for over $10,000, these printed directories could provide incomplete information for your situation. You will get to know your local sources through different avenues of research, which we cover later in this chapter.

The computerized publications of The Foundation Center database may be more helpful to you because they contain entries for a greater number of funders and grants. One version available only through on-line subscription contains the entire Foundation Center database. As of this writing the CD-ROM publication that contains the most listings is "FC Search" and is available to use free of charge in most Foundation Center libraries or collections.

→ Use a computerized database from The Foundation Center to generate one lead relevant to your organization, but don't spend hours looking up dozens of foundations. Print out the contact information for the funder you've discovered, or write it in here:

✍ Foundation: _____

✍ Contact name: _____

✍ Contact information: _____

Locally Published Guides to Funders. There are guides to funders for many states and larger communities, for example, the *Foundation Data Books* published for Oregon, Washington, Colorado, and California (www.foundationdatabook.com). For most small or new organizations a local or regional guide can provide most of the leads for your first several years of grant seeking. It will clue you in to foundations based in your community or state rather than turn up the Rockefellers and Carnegies.

Local guides may be published by your United Way, your public library, a government agency, or a private publisher. They vary widely in the quality and scope of information they contain; some states have guides that list every grant made by every foundation in the state on an annual basis. Some states we have seen list little more than the last known contact at each foundation. Most provide something in between.

→ Ask your librarian to help you find one or more local or regional guides to grant sources. Use the guide(s) to find one lead relevant to your organization. Photocopy the funder's contact information, or write it in here:

✍ Foundation: _____

✍ Contact name: _____

✍ Contact information: _____

If you cannot find a local guide to grant sources at the library, ask other grant seekers you know if they have one. Call the government office that regulates charities in your state (sometimes called the Charities Registrar and located in the secretary of state's office or the Department of Justice) and inquire about publications and databases relevant to grants in your community. As of this writing, the Maryland secretary of state's office maintains a list of Web links of charity regulation offices in other states at www.sos.state.md.us/sos/charity/html/otstates.html.

Newspapers and Trade Periodicals. We hope you're reading the newspaper and regional business journal on a regular basis because browsing through the morning papers can provide leads on funders and their situations. Foundation funding changes in response to corporate financial performance, mergers between businesses, and the stock market. These factors can and do have a bearing on how much grant funding is required to be paid out by foundations, where the decision-making staff or trustees will be located, and so on.

Your local papers are also valuable for keeping you up-to-date on philanthropic activity in your community. Occasionally there will be a story about a funder and its grant-making activities. More often there will be a story mentioning how a project was funded by a particular foundation or corporation.

While you're still at the library, make a more formal search of local and regional newspapers and business journals.

→ Ask the librarian to set you up with computer-based indexes of those publications. Try to find stories that will give you leads. For example, you could search for all the articles containing the words *trees, foundation,* and *grant.* Generate one lead this way. Print out the story or write what you've discovered in here:

Foundation: _____

Contact name: _____

Contact information: _____

Periodicals About Philanthropy. Your library may also hold periodicals about philanthropy in general, such as the *Chronicle of Philanthropy,* as well as periodicals for grant makers such as *Foundation News & Commentary.* You should get acquainted with these publications, read them as often as you can, and get your organization to subscribe to the ones you find most useful. *Chronicle of Philanthropy* regularly lists grants made by several foundations.

→ Ask your librarian to help you find back issues of *Chronicle of Philanthropy* and *Foundation News & Commentary.* (As of this writing the latter publication also has extensive archives available free on its Web site; the *Chronicle* site is fully available to paid subscribers.) Use one of these publications to generate one funding lead. Photocopy the relevant story or write what you've discovered in here:

Foundation: _____

Contact name: _____

Contact information: _____

Your day in the library is done. When you return to the office, you should have a small pile of photocopies, printouts, or notes that represent your leads. Take that pile and perform an essential piece of information management:

→ Drop all the leads you generated at the library into your "Funders to Contact" file.

Resist the urge to do more in-depth research on those leads right now. This is another exercise in the useful habit of dividing your time into blocks. You'll generate another set of leads first, and when you've got a significant number massed up, you'll follow up on all of them in one efficient work session.

Other Ways to Generate Leads

Back at the office there are more ways to get leads—some less obvious but potentially powerful.

Volunteers. Your organization probably has passionate volunteers, especially board and committee members, who work for corporations that have related foundations or corporate giving programs.

→ Introduce yourself to a couple of these volunteers. Find out what they do at your organization and why they enjoy doing it. Ask them if they have any ideas for funding your top-priority program. Generate one lead this way, and write it here:

✎ Foundation: _____

✎ Contact name: _____

✎ Contact information: _____

→ As usual drop a copy of this lead into your "Funders to Contact" folder.

Other Fundraisers You Know. You most likely know someone else who is a grant seeker, either paid or as a volunteer. If so call that person. Chat about projects you need to fund, and ask whether he or she has any interesting angles. Networking with your colleagues is a great source of information as well as support and celebration when you do receive funding.

If you don't know any other fundraisers, consider being brave and making a few calls to other nonprofit organizations' development departments. Introduce yourself as an educated novice looking for guidance. You may even strike up a conversation and ask your new colleague to meet with you. If you aren't already familiar with it, ask about your local development professional group or local chapter of the Association of Fundraising Professionals.

➜ Use your wits to locate the name and number of another serious grant seeker in your community, and write the person's name in here:

✍ _____

➜ Write in one lead generated by talking with a colleague:

✍ Foundation: _____

✍ Contact name: _____

✍ Contact information: _____

➜ Drop a copy of this lead into your "Funders to Contact" folder.

Periodicals. There are (sometimes pricey) publications and newsletters that specialize in announcing funding opportunities. Examples are *Nonprofit World Funding Alert* and *Corporate Grants Alert*. Publishers of these newsletters are often willing to send you free sample copies to determine whether they are right for you to purchase.

We recommend talking with your colleagues and librarians to narrow your list down to two or three possible newsletters before contacting the publishers for sample copies. You can also check out major publishers of these kinds of newsletters on the World Wide Web, including Aspen Publishers (www.aspenpub.com) and the Society for Nonprofit Organizations (http://danenet.wicip.org/snpo/).

Most recently some reliable "alert" newsletters have become available free through e-mail subscriptions. For example, the Foundation Center's weekly *RFP Bulletin* arrives by e-mail and contains over a dozen weekly grant announcements with links to relevant Web sites containing guidelines, application forms, and other announcements.

➜ By looking on the Web or calling a publisher or another grant seeker, get a complimentary or borrowed copy of one of these periodicals. Print out or photocopy one lead or write it in here:

✍ Foundation: _____

✍ Contact name: _____

✍ Contact information: _____

➜ Drop the lead in your "Funders to Contact" file.

The Internet. We saved this one for last because the Internet is a quickly changing medium, best used when you know which foundation you're looking for. The Internet can be a great time saver for getting basic documents like grant guidelines and application forms, and for conducting an in-depth investigation of funders, but you may need to invest time in learning what is out there. Simply surfing through foundation sites can be inefficient; you usually can't tell from a foundation's name whether it gives funding in your region or in your field of endeavor.

Increasing numbers of foundations are creating Web pages that include everything from their mission, overall initiatives, and basic grant guidelines to downloadable annual reports and application forms. (You often need Acrobat Reader, a free program from www.adobe.com, to read and print these documents.) Web pages maintained by the funders themselves are the most likely to contain accurate information about their current guidelines and grant-making activities, so we'll start there.

➜ Go to a well-respected site such as the *Chronicle of Philanthropy* (www.philanthropy.com) or the *Council on Foundations* (www.cof.org). Follow the site's links to foundations' Web sites and find one foundation lead relevant to your organization. Print out the contact information or write it in here:

✍ Foundation: _____

✍ Web address: _____

➜ Bookmark the site and drop the lead into your "Funders to Contact" folder.

Right now your main purpose is to get leads, so don't get too involved in reading everything on all these Web sites you find. You'll do more research using the Web later.

Paid Search Services. Finally, there are (sometimes expensive) paid on-line search services that do some of the work for you, based on parameters you provide such as keywords like "opera" and "Cincinnati." If you are just beginning in grants, we recommend you become familiar with the free information at your library and on the Web before you consider paying for search services. Although a search service may ultimately be right for you, the free stuff may be enough to keep you occupied for your first year or more.

By this point you should have a collection of at least ten leads in your "Funders to Contact" file. Don't stay at work all night generating millions more. Go home for a rest, or go out for a beer or coffee. You already know that grant seeking is a long-term process, not a quick fix. You want a steady, evolving effort, so pace yourself.

GETTING BASIC INFORMATION ABOUT YOUR LEADS

Now that you have some leads, you need to obtain basic information from all those potential funders—their application guidelines and forms and their most recent annual reports. Although 90 percent of the time this task will be perfunctory, it sometimes provides the opportunity for your first personal contact with a funder. That personal contact can make a difference, so you need to be a little prepared for it.

➜ Set aside a specific hour out of your work week to remove all your new leads from the "Funders to Contact" file and contact them. This work is repetitive and is most efficiently done in chunks.

➜ Before you contact any of them, write a one-sentence description of your organization and the project you are seeking to fund in language you could easily say over the phone. An example would be, "We're an innovative food bank and nutrition organization seeking to expand our services to rural areas."

→ Similarly, write out three points you'd like people to know about your program in language you could say naturally over the phone. An example would be, "Our food bank preserves our clients' dignity."

_____

Now you're ready to contact your leads, asking for their publications such as guidelines, application forms, and annual reports. Of course for some funders you may be able to get these documents from their Web sites with no personal interaction whatsoever. It's the e-mail and phone methods that provide more of an opportunity and more of a risk. Occasionally the person at the other end will engage you in conversation. This is your opportunity to interest a potential funder in your organization and your project. That person may respond with interest and give you information that will steer your proposal in the right direction.

The risk is that you don't know much about the grant makers you talk to, because you are calling to get their materials and so haven't studied them yet. You may talk about something that turns out to be outside their area of interest, leading them to disqualify you before they've seen your full proposal. You don't want that to happen.

If you use e-mail to request basic information, create a short, generic message that you can save in your e-mail "Drafts" folder and use again and again. In that message give your one-sentence description of your organization and project. There's a possibility this description will stick in someone's mind and help you later. Ask that the person e-mail or mail the materials to you or steer you to the appropriate Web site. And remember to say thank you. That's it.

Most of the time you will get a nearly automatic response, but occasionally the response might be a request for more information about your program. If you feel you are ready, you can use this as an opportunity to start a working relationship with the funder and send your ideas. For example, you might send your three talking points. If you are uncomfortable with this risk, you can let your contact person know that you are doing very preliminary grant research. Ask whether you might talk more later, after you have read the funder's annual report and are more familiar with their grant making. Although in the short term you may lose one e-mail opportunity, you will likely gain respect and credibility that will pay off in the long run when you are ready with a proposal. An alternative, if you do not feel ready for conversation about your program, is to refer the contact person's questions to your CEO.

If you use the telephone the scenario is similar. Most of the time you will be talking to a receptionist, or you may be sent to a voice mailbox; it is unlikely that you'll be asked about your program. However, you may get a program officer or trustee on the phone. Do be prepared to give a one-sentence description of your project, just in case you are asked about it. If the person engages you in positive conversation, that is the best! But the key is that you don't want to have your chances for a grant made or broken on this first call.

Having said all that, we must tell you that in 90 percent of cases all you'll get to do is leave your name and address.

Some foundations don't give out their phone numbers or have Web sites, so you'll have to write them to request their publications and guidelines. If you must write, do so as a last resort because it is the most time-consuming way to get the information you need. Send only a short, generic letter making your request. Resist the urge to start describing your program in this letter. You do not want to be turned down for a grant at this stage, before you even see the foundation's materials and make a proper match with your programs. Save your request note on your computer so you can use it as a template for future letters of this kind.

Now that you've been debriefed on the fine art of this peculiar stage of grant seeking, get some practice doing it.

→ Spend an hour making inquiries about your ten leads using e-mail, the Web, the phone, and U.S. mail.

→ When you're finished making inquiries, place your leads in your "Folders to Make" area. We'll explain this filing move shortly.

MANAGING INFORMATION OVERLOAD

Soon after you make your inquiries about your leads (perhaps only a few minutes if you're downloading material from the Web), you'll have to start dealing with information overload. Guidelines, annual reports, and other documents from funders start to land in volume on your desk, as well as other items you've requested during your organization and community research: budgets and plans from your organization's program staff, government reports, and so on. These are in addition to all the documents you're creating and the memos that are part of any office job.

You deal with so much information, at least half of it printed on paper, that filing is more than just a nice idea. You need to file to survive—to keep from being overwhelmed and unfocused. Filing regularly is the number one way to engage in another important habit of efficient grant seeking: clearing your workspaces of papers and objects that confuse or distract you from what you are doing. Filing allows your office to physically reflect the straightforward and intelligent mind-set you apply to grant seeking, and it helps you divide your time into useful blocks, working on just one proposal or project at a time without being reminded of others that are lurking around in various boxes and piles on your desk.

You also need to file consistently and clearly because grant seeking is rarely a solo operation. Other people at your organization are going to need access to your papers, sometimes on very short notice (for example, when a funder calls with a question). It will be hard for them to find what they need in piles of paper on your desk, but it will be easy for them to remember something like "If the grant seeker isn't using it, it's in the file cabinet, filed under the funder's name."

So when material arrives on your desk or in your electronic in-box, deal with it in a reasonable, time-conscious way. Don't interrupt your work or lose your focus. But don't let it pile up too long. We recommend filing away papers the same day you use them. Although we do advocate having a few special temporary holding places for certain kinds of information such as the "Funders to Contact" folder we used in this chapter, resist the temptation to label a box "To File" and then dump everything in the world into it.

The same principles apply to filing on your computer. Keep on top of your electronic files, taking time each day or week to empty your e-mail in-box and relocate any files that have been saved in the wrong places. Back in Chapter Three you created computer folders that mirror your paper folders. For example, you made a folder for community information in general, with detail folders for research, news clippings, and so on. You might want to do your electronic filing at the same time you do your paper filing.

It should be simple to file community- and organization-related materials you receive, because in Chapter Three you made a whole set of folders for those subjects.

→ After scanning them quickly, file community and organizational materials in the appropriate locations. You can study the materials in more detail when you are working on relevant tasks.

Materials like guidelines and annual reports that funders send out are a little trickier. There are so many funders that you are less likely to have a file already created for each one whose materials you receive. And you may want to study these documents in the near future to check for upcoming funding opportunities. So put these materials in a special holding place.

→ When materials from funders arrive, don't interrupt your work. Do put them immediately in the file, "To Read and Consider."

→ Set aside one or two hours per week to review all the materials in that file.

SCREENING LEADS AND MAKING FOLDERS

When the time comes to review the materials in "To Read and Consider," do so carefully. This is your first screening of the potential funders you've discovered. Your goal is to get a strong sense of what the funders' mission, requirements, and practices are. You don't need to read every sentence, especially of lengthy annual reports, but if you skim too quickly and fail to perceive important information, you will waste time later by going back over the same material again and again. Here are some tips for what to look for and highlight:

→ Write today's date (including the year) on the front of the guidelines so that when you look at them a few months or years from now you'll know how old they are.

→ Highlight any deadlines.

→ Flag any pages that list instructions for applying for a grant, and flag any application forms and checklists they provide.

→ Highlight any relevant text about their values, interests, and mission.

→ Highlight anything that disqualifies your organization for funding. Examples might be geographic limits, restrictions on United Way agencies, restrictions on grants for certain types of activities such as religious programs, publications, or conferences, and so on. Be sure to highlight if a funder's materials say they do not accept unsolicited proposals.

If you find you are *not* eligible for a grant:

→ Note your ineligibility on the front of the materials.

→ Drop the materials into the "Folders to Make" folder. (Don't neglect this step. We'll explain it shortly.)

If the guidelines indicate that you are ineligible, believe it. Resist trying to twist the rules or bend your program in your mind to make it eligible. In a survey of corporate grant makers published in her book *Fistfuls of Dollars: Fact and Fantasy About Corporate Charitable Giving,* Linda Zukowski reports that 40 to 90 percent of proposals were immediately rejected because they didn't fit the giving guidelines.[2] As an efficient grant seeker you realize it is a poor use of your time to try to get a grant for which you're not eligible. Why not spend your time where you have the best chance of funding instead?

If you *are* eligible:

→ Finish reviewing the funder's information.

→ Write out a deadline card for each of the funder's deadlines, and place it in your "Deadline" file.

A *deadline card,* as you may recall from Chapter Three, is simply an index card with a funder's name and a deadline date on it, for example, "ABC Foundation, proposals due June 30." These cards go in the "Deadline" file in chronological order. Here are some important points about deadline cards. Use one card for each deadline. If the XYZ Foundation has deadlines of January 1 and July 1, make two cards. Do not include the year unless the deadline applies to only one year (for example, a one-time request for proposals or a foundation that changes its due dates each year). Most funders' deadlines repeat year after year, and your deadline cards can be used over and over.

If a funder has multilevel deadlines, make a card for each. For example, if a funder requires a pre-proposal letter, often called a letter of inquiry, by January 1 and full proposals by June 1, make two cards but write "Inquiry" or some other note on the January card, and make a note on the June card that it is by invitation only. Resist the temptation to add other notes and ideas to the cards. You (or your organization) will be using these cards year after year, and in the future you don't want to get confused by obsolete notes.

If a funder does not have deadlines, you still need to make a deadline card, but you have two choices about how to do it. You can write something like "Ongoing" on the card and give it its own section in the "Deadline" file, or you can create an artificial deadline for yourself. The latter will work best if you have a specific grant proposal in mind, but the "Ongoing" note will work best if you don't know yet what you're going to do.

When you are finished making the funder's deadline cards, do this:

→ Drop the funder's material into your "Folders to Make" area.
→ Repeat this screening process for all your leads.

Making Needed File Folders

The "Folders to Make" area is a temporary holding place reserved for material you know you want to keep but does not yet have a dedicated file folder, such as the funder guidelines you just reviewed. This material accumulates as you work. To keep from being overwhelmed and disorganized, you need to make new folders to hold this material. But because making new folders is repetitive and time consuming, you should do this:

→ Set aside chunks of time for making new file folders.
→ During those times remove everything from the "Folders to Make" area, make folders for all the funders, and then file all the materials appropriately.

You might have noticed that we asked you to make folders for and file *all* the materials you've reviewed. This includes funders for whom you are *not* eligible. Experience has taught us there are at least two good reasons to file that material: (1) as time goes by and you are swamped with information, it is easy to forget that you have inquired with a funder or the reasons you were ineligible; and (2) in the future your organization or the funder's guidelines may change, and you could become eligible.

CONGRATULATIONS

Time to wipe your brow and crack open a beverage. You've reached the end of Step One of the grant-seeking cycle. You can be relieved that Step One will never take this long again. You've learned a lot about your community, your organization, and your potential funders. Now it's time to put all that information together into an inspiring fusion of interests. You'll do this in "Step Two: Match Your Request to Your Funder."

Match Your
Request to
a Funder

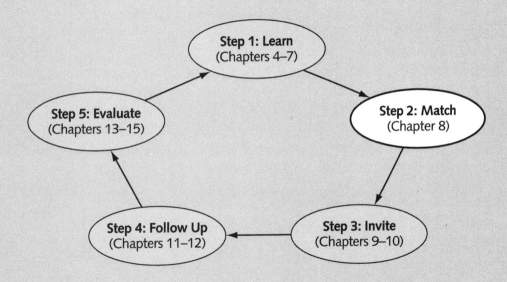

Next you match your organization's programs and needs with a
particular funder's giving patterns and mission. Out of your organization's many needs, you determine which ones the funder will
find most interesting. Your goal is to move beyond a mere compatibility with a funder to discover the specific things they will
find compelling and natural to fund. By the end of Step Two, you
know exactly what you will ask for.

Move from Lead to Prospect to Match

People in theater say success is 90 percent casting. They mean that if you have the right actors, the presentation of the play becomes easier and more natural, resulting in a production that seems elegant and effortless, almost meant to be. In grant seeking the match is similarly important. The match is the convergence of your organization's programs and financial needs, your community's needs, and a funder's interests and resources. If the match is right, presenting it in the form of a proposal becomes easier. A great match is one that seems so natural that the funder gets excited about your invitation to give.

To imagine a simple and good match, consider a small, fictional foundation that is interested in women's issues. The foundation rarely gives grants of more than a few thousand dollars, and an application can be made in a simple letter. The foundation has a quick response rate, sending out grant funds within six weeks of receiving requests. This funder would be a good match if your organization's women's health clinic had an emergency and needed a new furnace; that's the kind of project that matches with the funder's personality and past giving. The foundation also responds quickly enough to meet an emergency need. However, if you need to build a whole new clinic, there would be no point in asking this funder for hundreds of thousands of dollars to build it. Even though the foundation clearly supports work in your field, it just doesn't give away that kind of money.

Finding the right match is perhaps the most important part of a grant seeker's job—more important than writing. It combines your knowledge with your intuition and creativity, so it can be fun. Although there's certainly an art to finding a match, many of the key elements can be identified.

We conceive a good match as having four parts. First, there must be an overall *mission match and eligibility,* which you determined during your recent screening session. For example, you and your prospective funder might have a common interest in women's issues. Next there must be a match among the funder's interests, the community's needs, and a *specific project* of yours—converging, for example, in your women's health clinic. Within that program or project there is often a specific *element or angle* to highlight that will appeal most to a particular funder—for example, to buy a furnace that meets the immediate needs of clinic patients for basic comfort. Finally, there is the *cash amount* of your request, which should fit with the funder's giving history and guidelines.

You build a match based on everything you know about the organization, community, and prospective funder. You already know a lot about the first two subjects, and you've been downloading and receiving materials from your funding leads to get to know more about each of them. You've screened each lead for eligibility. We call the funders for whom you are eligible your *prospects.* In this chapter we'll study one of your prospects intensively to try to find a good match and to give you experience in thinking about the many ingredients that make or break a good approach to a funder. As you become experienced with grant seeking and get to know the foundations you work with frequently, this process will become quicker and more intuitive. For now, though, we'll walk you through step by step.

WALKING THROUGH A MATCH

The first part of making a match is picking a funder to analyze.

→ Of all the prospects you found in Chapter Seven, choose one for more intensive study. (Just pick the one that sounds best so far; you don't need to agonize over this decision.)

→ Find a source of detailed information about your prospect's past giving, such as its annual report or recent federal tax return.

The tax returns of private foundations list grants paid during the tax year in question, usually as an attachment toward the back of the return. They also list the names of the foundation's trustees during that tax year. Tax returns can be an excellent source of straightforward information about a funder's giving patterns, as long as you remember a funder's return may be from two or more years ago; their policies and trustees may have changed in the meantime.

People new to grant seeking sometimes resist looking at tax returns, feeling that they're prying or being sneaky. We urge you to let go of those feelings. Looking at a foundation's tax return is an accepted part of doing your homework. In March 2000 this practice was formalized through legislation that directs private foundations in the United States to make their tax returns available to anyone on written request.

You might be relieved to learn that getting access to those tax returns is an impersonal process. Almost every private foundation's tax return—its 990-PF—can be obtained on the Internet at www.GrantSmart.org, www.guidestar.org or possibly through your state's Charities Registrar, which we discuss in the last chapter. Even if you have a detailed annual report issued by your prospect, it's not a bad idea to get practice retrieving and reading 990-PFs.

→ Locate GrantSmart.org or guidestar.org and download your prospect's most recent tax return.

Now you can look at your prospect's actual giving. For example, how big were this foundation's grants? Did the foundation tend to give more to certain geographic areas or types of programs? What programs of yours seem to match best? For the rest of this chapter we'll list the kind of questions you can ask yourself about a funder to help construct a match. These questions also appear in Exhibit A.3 (in Resource A).

To ground these questions in an example, we've written up the notes of a fictional grant seeker from a fictional wildlife protection organization. This grant seeker is looking for a match with a fictional foundation called the Raptor Rescue Fund.

Funder's Capacity to Give

Some of the easiest, most concrete facts to glean from funders' Web sites, annual reports, and tax returns are the dollar amounts of the grants they make. This is important information to study. You may have heard about a $1-million grant your prospect made, or you may have read in the newspaper about several $100,000 grants your prospect gave to local nonprofits working in a particular field. But these may be exceptions to the foundation's normal or typical giving. Without some focused research you might not know that and might approach the foundation for a totally inappropriate amount of money.

The appropriateness of your approach to a funder is critical. A mistake beginners often make is to ask for the moon, thinking something like, "They have so much money, we should ask for a million," or "They'll give us half the amount we request, so we should ask high." This approach can be damaging. If you ask for a grant that is far above a foundation's grant range, it will be immediately apparent to them that you haven't done your homework, and your proposal may seem thoughtless or even greedy. However, if you ask for a grant that is too far under a foundation's typical grant range, you may fall right off their radar screen.

You can keep this from happening by determining the right amount to request from a particular funder. As you look at the sources you've gathered that detail your prospect's past giving, ask yourself questions like these:

✔ What is this foundation's grant range? What is its average grant amount in dollars? How many grants did it make last year?

✔ What percentage of these grants were given to organizations or programs similar to ours? In our geographic area?

✔ Of those grants given to organizations similar to ours, what is the average grant amount? This figure may differ significantly from the overall average and will give you a clue as to what amount to apply for.

If you were a grant seeker from a wildlife protection organization, looking for a match with the fictional Raptor Rescue Fund, here is how your notes might read:

Funder: Raptor Rescue Fund. Grant stats: $500 to $10,000; average grant $8,000. They make about 12 grants per year, 100 percent to organizations like ours across the U.S. No geographic area seems to receive any special focus.

Your History with the Funder

Another consideration is how well this funder knows your organization. The more trust and respect the funder has for your organization and the better its past experiences with you have been, the more appropriate it may be for you to push the higher end of the funder's grant range. It's important to imagine life on the other side of the table, that is, how the staff and trustees of a foundation might react to your grant request. You should ask yourself whether your history warrants a higher-level request being seriously considered.

Recall the example from Chapter One. You might give a personal donation of $1 to practically anyone's cause, with few questions asked and little expectation of return. For $100 your standards would probably be more selective; you might expect to see receipts or at least receive a thank-you letter and some proof that the money went to good use. For $10,000 you might even require a contract and follow-up report.

Foundations and corporations are similar in that they have comfort levels and standards that apply to their grant making; each one's comfort level is unique. We have received grants of $25,000 through the mail without any personal contact and no prior experience with the funders. And we have worked with funders who took several years to learn about our organizations and our work standards before giving us $10,000 grants.

Funders might learn about you from having made previous grants to your organization; they might note how you followed up on those grants, as well as the quality of their experience working with your board members and staff. Evidence of these situations may exist in your organization's files. Earlier we asked you to set aside any existing grant files to set up your new system. Now go back to those files, if any, and check whether there is one for the foundation you're currently considering.

Think about the prospect you're studying and use any existing files. Then ask yourself questions like these:

✔ Has this foundation made any grants to our organization over the past five years? If so what were their amounts, and what were they for?

✔ Did we complete all the grant requirements on time, including required reports?

✔ Are there any notes in our files about conversations our staff members had with foundation staff or trustees? If so is there any indication of what the foundation would like to see next from our organization?

✔ Are there names of foundation people in our files to call for guidance or ideas? Is there any evidence that one of our board members knows anyone at this foundation?

If you were a grant seeker from a wildlife protection organization who is looking for a match with the fictional Raptor Rescue Fund, here is how your notes might read:

Raptor Rescue Fund gave us $5,000 in 1998 for Take a Raptor to School Day. We sent a final report on time, and our project met its goals. There are no specific notes on any contact among our trustees and this funder. The file lists Stan Allan, the program officer, as our last contact. Evan, our founder, knows a trustee.

Funder's Current Grant-Making Focus

Each foundation has a mission, along with initiatives to make that mission come to life, just the way your organization does. You want to approach a foundation with a project that will help fulfill the foundation's mission and meet its goals. Not only will this position you best for funding but it will also communicate that you respect the funder's time.

So look at your prospect's Web site, guidelines, and past grants, and ask yourself a few questions about its grant-making focus:

✔ Why did I think of this foundation in the first place?

✔ What do they say they are interested in funding? Given my research, what is my impression about what this funder gives the most money to? Does it differ from, or is it more focused or broader than, their stated interests?

✔ If this foundation has given to causes or organizations similar to ours recently, which ones were they?

✔ From what I've learned so far and given my organization's fundraising priorities, what project of ours seems to match best with this prospect's grant making?

If you were a grant seeker from a wildlife protection organization, looking for a match with the fictional Raptor Rescue Fund, here is how your notes might read:

I thought of Raptor Rescue Fund because we had a previous grant from them, and their mission matches with our programs for injured wild birds.

Their materials say they fund "Programs that save raptors and return them to the wild or educate the public about raptors." It seems like they give 50 percent or more to education, even though "rescue" is their name. Actual grants on their tax return indicate more stress on education than their guidelines state.

Recently they've given to a public school wild bird education project, a Wild Bird Sanctuary trail project, and two other raptor rescue programs in other states.

We could ask them to fund direct rescue of injured birds or a public education campaign. It seems like the latter fits better, and both are equal needs for us.

Angle of Approach

As we've discussed, most foundations don't want to be the sole funder of a program or project. Sometimes they will accept a proposal describing a whole project, understanding that their funding will cover a certain percentage of the total budget without requiring you to specify which pieces their dollars will pay for. This will almost always be preferable to you, because it allows you the most flexibility with grant dollars.

At other times, though, funders will require you to note exactly which elements of your budget will be paid for with their grant. Or in light of your research results you may feel you would strengthen your proposal by asking for a grant to cover a specific piece of your whole budget. For example, you might ask a corporate foundation that is set up by a publishing company to fund the cost of books for your new literacy program.

By now you've thought about your prospect's giving history, mission, and experience with your organization, as well as which project of yours seems to make the most sense to bring to this funder. Now you need to decide, given all this information, exactly what element of your project you will stress and exactly what grant amount you will propose.

Remember that grants are generally made for new programs, expansions, and capital purchases rather than for ongoing, regular expenses. These items, which are most often considered by foundation funders, are sometimes called grant-worthy because they are the most likely to garner grant funding.

Within these overall parameters each funder will have its own guidelines and preferences. Some may prefer to focus on physical items such as coats for children or garden seeds; whereas others will consider all the expenses of a new or expanding program, from postage to insurance. Funders may have specific prohibitions. A few we've seen include no funding for conferences, publications, food, or staff salaries. At this stage during your match making, it's important for you to review any specific statements the funder has made about what pieces of a program's budget it will and won't consider paying for.

Think about your first-priority program and ask yourself this:

✔ Does our program have any specific grant-worthy needs at this time? How much do each of our needed items cost?

Record your needs as though they were a shopping list, including projected prices (which you received during your interview with your program director). There's room for your shopping list on the Considering a Match form in Exhibit A.3.

If you were a grant seeker from a wildlife protection organization, looking for a match with the fictional Raptor Rescue Fund, here is how your shopping list might read:

Shopping List for Public Education Campaign

Program Needs	Costs
Web design	$3,000
Print materials	$2,000
Advertising space (print)	$10,000
Advertising time (radio)	$50,000
Public service announcement taping	$9,000

After making your shopping list do some further analysis. Ask yourself these questions:

✔ Do any of the amounts on our list match or come close to the average grants this foundation made to organizations similar to ours last year?

✔ Do any of the items seem especially appropriate or inappropriate, given our prospect's overall interests, past grant making (to our organization and others), and guidelines (for example, they might not fund salaries)?

✔ Do any of the items stand out as cohesive, self-contained concepts that I could easily communicate to someone? Are any more exciting or appealing than others or far more crucial to the success of the project?

It may take some time to mull these questions over. When you're done:

➜ Circle the item or items on your list that make the best match.

If you were a grant seeker from a wildlife protection organization, looking for a match with the fictional Raptor Rescue Fund, here is how your notes might read:

Within our public education program, PSA taping and ad space seem about the right amounts, given their record.

PSA taping seems to fit well with this funder's interest in direct public education and with their actual grant making. The PSA is more fun and interesting and less like overhead than the advertising. I could make a better case for it, I think.

Shopping List for Public Education Campaign

Program Needs	Costs
Web design	$3,000
Print materials	$2,000
Advertising space (print)	$10,000
Advertising time (radio)	$50,000
Public service announcement taping	$9,000

Timing of Proposal

If you've been following the example responses to this exercise, you probably detected a grant-seeking "angle" developing. The imaginary grant seeker is thinking something like, "I want to apply to the Raptor Rescue Fund to meet some of my organization's current needs. They seem to stress education in their giving. Out of all our needs, the thing that might appeal to the funder most would be supporting our PSA taping for $9,000. It's not out of line with the money they've spent in the past on us and on this issue, so I'm going to go ahead and ask for it." You may be reaching a similar conclusion with your prospect or realizing that the prospect is not so good after all—a perfectly valid and useful result of this matching process.

If your match is looking good, you'll want to ask yourself some more questions to dig for the kind of details that can make your proposal seem especially timely and relevant to the funder. Ask yourself these questions:

✔ Given our needs, our history with this funder, and the funder's giving timeline, why is it time to ask for a grant now? Is the timing strategic for our organization? For the community? For this particular funder?

✔ What do I feel is the best approach we can take? Does the foundation have a deadline coming up? Do they request proposals by mail only? Do I have a reason I can call first? Does this funder require or request a letter of inquiry first before taking any phone calls or full proposals?

✔ Does something about our project warrant an in-person visit or tour? For example, is our request especially large, or does our proposal represent a major change in the level of this funder's involvement with us?

If you were a grant seeker from a wildlife protection organization, looking for a match with the fictional Raptor Rescue Fund, here is how your notes might read:

The application deadline is March 1. That's 3 weeks away. A grant could make a big difference for us right now, because we need our PSA made by November. That's when the governor is going to declare Raptor Day and make a speech about wild bird protection.

I think I should call and meet the funders if possible, since we have some history with them, but not much. This proposal would almost double our last grant from them. It sounds like a good time to invite them for a tour of our place.

They request a full proposal using their form, but there's no stipulation against calling first.

DO YOU HAVE A MATCH?

If you came up with a natural match, congratulations! You are ready to ask this funder to give to your program, and you'll do so in the next chapter, as you start Step Three.

→ To remind yourself and others that you are officially working on a grant request with this funder, find or create the deadline card for this grant opportunity and tack it up on your bulletin board.

If you didn't have quite as much success in forming a conclusion as our fictional grant seeker did, that's okay. In fact, if you found no plausible base for a match, you've had a valuable experience. You won't waste any time writing a proposal to this funder at this time. However, in order to progress within this book, you do need to make a good match before moving on to the next chapter. So if you didn't find a match this time, do this:

→ Go back through your entire list of prospects. Using the Considering a Match form to guide you, research and evaluate your prospects until you have defined at least one solid match to use through the next several chapters. When you've found it, tack the deadline card up on the bulletin board.

step three **Invite** a Funder to Invest in Your Organization

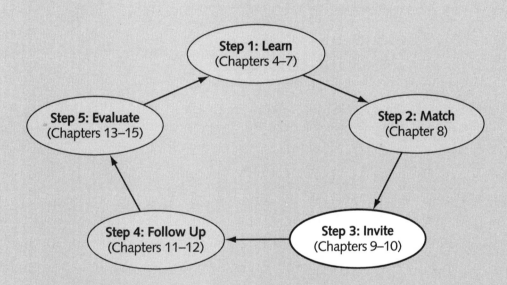

Now that you have identified a match with a prospective funder, you invite the funder to invest in your organization by giving you a grant. You might make this invitation by writing a full grant proposal, but the invitation could begin with a simple phone call, letter of inquiry, or face-to-face meeting.

Invite a Funder to Give

Step Three of the grant-seeking cycle is where you ask your prospective funder for money. Don't rush to fire up your word processing program to write a *full grant proposal,* though, because that is just one of five basic ways you can make your initial contact. Other options are to make an *introductory phone call,* request a *meeting* with the funder, set up a *site visit* by the funder, or write a *letter of inquiry.* Depending on your situation, you may use any or all of these five methods as you make your request.

In this chapter we'll discuss the various ways of making contact with a funder and communicating your formal request for a grant. Then we'll cover exactly how to make an introductory phone call and write a grant proposal or letter of inquiry. Because you may not get a meeting or a site visit before you submit your proposal in writing, we'll save those topics for the next chapter.

DECIDING ON YOUR INITIAL APPROACH

You have both short- and long-terms goals as you initiate your grant request. You obviously want to get the grant you are currently seeking. Given the fact that there is likely a gigantic stack of grant applications at the funder's office, it's in your interest to raise the funder's consciousness about and confidence in your organization and its programs. In addition to the grant at hand, you want to establish and cultivate a working relationship that will lead to recurring and increasing numbers of grants from your prospect, as well as respect for your organization in the grant-making community. You'd like to get your application near the top of everyone's stack. At the same time you need to respect funders' guidelines and practices, as well as the time of each funder's staff people.

Unless your prospect's guidelines say not to do this, you will want to lay some groundwork with an introductory phone call or perhaps an equivalent e-mail. This call takes up little time and can be valuable for all involved. It gives you a chance to introduce your project and perhaps test your match with the funder; it gives the funder the opportunity to conduct a quick screening of your organization's and program's basic eligibility. The call also gives you an opportunity to ask questions. Perhaps the language in the funder's guidelines is vague, and you are really not sure whether you qualify for that funder's grants; perhaps you don't understand what kind of detail is needed in the proposal budget.

As the foundation representative responds, you will probably gain some valuable information that is not in the published guidelines. You might be surprised to find that foundation staff often want to assist you rather than put you off. After all, it's part of their job and their goal to help you make appropriate requests that may turn into successful grants. Funders focused on working with new, small non-profits may be accustomed to helping potential grantees with little experience in grant seeking. Most funders should be interested in talking with you, at least to discourage any inappropriate proposals.

Whether the information you gain during a phone call is positive ("We're concentrating in that area this year"), negative ("We don't fund that anymore"), or simply practical ("Send the application in before June because that's when funding decisions are made"), it should help you target your work.

An initial phone call also gives you the chance to ask the funder for a face-to-face meeting (at the funder's office) or a site visit (the funder comes to your site). You may want to ask for a meeting or visit, based on a few factors such as your history with the prospect, the likelihood that the funder has a good impression of your organization already, and any current events that affect your relationship.

Some grant-seeking experts might advise you to strive for a meeting or visit with *every* potential funder. This idea is based on the tenets of sales and fundraising that face-to-face contact results in more positive response and that grants are made and lost on the basis of personal encounters.

Although we can't deny the merit in these ideas—for example, certain meetings could be crucial to increasing a foundation staff member's confidence in your organization—we think the desirability of meetings is misunderstood within the world of small and mid-size foundation grants. At specific times you will want to propose meetings with funders and persist until you achieve them. But just as often you won't need to meet and can simply mail a good proposal without fanfare. For a rural nonprofit, where it was difficult and time consuming to meet with foundation representatives in the city, we won grants of up to $25,000 and raised about 10 percent of our organization's budget using only the U.S. mail. And from organizations we already had business relationships with (not always 100 percent positive ones), we've gotten grants of up to $250,000, as well as one in-kind grant worth $1.25 million, through introductory phone calls and written proposals; we had no special meetings or tours.

We don't think asking for a meeting or tour is always necessary or even a good idea because encounters without a clear purpose can be disrespectful of everyone's time. In certain circumstances—for example, a grant of $2,000 from a funder that makes dozens of small grants each year—any personal contact beyond a telephone call may be overkill. Even for more sizable requests, meetings arranged merely for the sake of getting face time often turn into bland encounters where the funding representative reiterates the published guidelines, and you smile and send a thank-you note. We doubt these kinds of meetings do much to advance a real working relationship or communicate intangible qualities like trustworthiness.

We propose what might be considered a radical approach: try to get a meeting only when you have a reason for one. Your reason may be as simple as introducing yourself and your new program. Your job is to decide whether you have a reason that warrants a meeting, to know the premise for your meeting, and to communicate that to your colleagues who attend. (We'll cover this in more detail in Chapter Ten.) There are many good premises for meetings; you just need to have one. Consider a few:

- Your organization is brand new or new to the community in which you're seeking grants, and you need to establish your identity with a funder.
- Your organization is new to a funder and is not well known in the community, so there is a good likelihood the funder has never heard of you.

- Your program is hard to describe on paper, or you are excellent at describing it in person but have difficulty writing about it well.

- There has been a significant staff change at your organization, and somebody new (the new CEO, board president, or you—the new grants person) wants an introduction to the funder.

- There has been a staff or trustee change at a foundation with which you already work.

- You are thinking of proposing a change in the magnitude or character of a funder's relationship with your organization, for example, by asking a funder to go from giving $10,000 annual gifts to making a three-year commitment of $300,000.

- The funder has had mixed or negative experiences with your organization in the past. For example, you might have been late in turning in required progress reports, and you need to reassure the funder that you take its support seriously.

- You want a foundation representative's advice in how to make requests to other funders, or you are asking a foundation representative to review a draft proposal for a major project.

- You have a genuine need for assistance with or clarification of funder guidelines or application forms that cannot be handled over the phone.

Similarly, you should ask for a site visit by a funder only if you have a reason for it. This takes up even more of everyone's time, so besides substantial issues to discuss, there should be something to see other than an office space—something that can be communicated most effectively in person. Here are some examples:

- You have a program participant, such as a child and his or her mentor, for the funder to (briefly) meet.

- You have a visually captivating and active program, such as a community garden in full bloom or a theater space with an interesting set in place.

- You are applying for a capital project such as a new day care center, where the cramped present-day conditions make a visual case for funding.

After weighing all these thoughts, look again at your prospect's guidelines. Then do this:

➜ Make your decision about how to approach the funder, whether it will be through a phone call, meeting, site visit, letter of inquiry, full proposal, or some combination thereof. (Keep in mind that even with a meeting or visit, a letter or proposal will nearly always be required. You will get your chance to create one later in this chapter.)

Don't be surprised if, after you decide to ask for a meeting or a visit, the notion turns out to be moot. Some funders are glad to meet with prospective grantees, but you'll find that the majority are not easily accessible. Many funders have policies that prohibit meetings before written materials are submitted. This may be their way of dealing with information overload or an attempt to remain fair and objective; you should not take this kind of policy as a rejection. Although funders use written materials to screen out applicants, remember that you chose this funder because you had evidence that you'd found a good match with your programs. Your research has already shown that the foundation funds your kind of organization and project. Because you are prepared and focused, it's unlikely that you'll be screened out prematurely.

MAKING AN INTRODUCTORY CALL

If you've followed the exercises in this book, you should be more than ready to talk about your top-priority program with an interested foundation officer. However, you may be more confident and coherent on the phone if you prepare yourself a little.

Recall the one-sentence description of your organization and project, along with the three points you'd like people to know about them, that you created in Chapter Seven. Now that you'll be talking to the staff or trustees of a *particular* funder, which you researched in some detail in Chapter Eight, you may want to revise those talking points somewhat. Write them here in language you can easily say over the phone:

➜ Write a one-sentence description of your program and project (for example, "We're an innovative food bank and nutrition organization, seeking to expand our services to rural areas").

 _____

Write three points you'd like people to know about your project (for example, "Our food bank preserves people's dignity").

 _____

_____

_____

You may be calling simply to introduce yourself and your idea. Or you may have some questions you need clarified, which can help give purpose and structure to your call. Perhaps you have an intelligent question about the funder's application form; perhaps you want to check in before applying for something unusual, given your previous relationship; perhaps you want to request a meeting or site visit.

➔ If it helps you to do so, write in your questions or purpose here:

 _____

Now you're ready for your next step:

➔ Call the funder you are interested in.

Don't assume anything about the first person you reach on the phone. You may have reached a temporary employee who is filling in as receptionist, or you may have reached a decision maker right off the bat, especially if you are calling a smaller foundation. Express the purpose of your call; if you haven't reached the right person, ask with whom you should speak. You may need to call a few times to reach this person, but persistence (not nagging) can leave a good impression.

When you get to the right person, your goal is to communicate your idea and get answers to your questions. Of course you want to make a positive and professional impression along the way. Don't forget to introduce yourself and your organization briefly—for example, with your one-sentence description. As we explained before, you may be pleasantly surprised at grant makers' willingness to help you, but if they put you off, there's no point in getting upset. It's not personal.

If your goal is to arrange a meeting, ask for twenty or thirty minutes of the funder's time so that your organization's CEO (and a board member you know is willing) can come to the office to discuss your organization's mission and grant-worthy project. Remember that a site visit, if you're asking for one, will take up even more time, so you should be confident it will be worth the potential funder's while.

What to Do if the Funder Says Yes

If you have successfully set up a personal meeting with the funder, skip to Chapter Ten, where we discuss meetings and tours. When the time comes to submit written materials, come back to this chapter for a discussion of proposals and letters of inquiry.

What to Do if the Funder Says No

With dozens or even hundreds of requests a week, it isn't surprising that most funders will say no to your request for a personal meeting. Don't get angry or frustrated. Your phone call can still function as a valuable introduction to or reminder about your organization. Your aim at this point is to get any advice or information about sending written materials. Consider asking one or two questions you have about their guidelines or grant-making process.

How to End the Call

End the call by thanking the person for any information he or she has given you, and say that you will get a proposal in under the next deadline or by a date you choose for yourself if one is not specified. But remember that when you make such a statement, you create an expectation about yourself. Make sure it is an expectation you can fulfill.

➔ Create deadline cards for any promises you've made, such as "We'll send a proposal by XYZ" or "We'll call you again after the end of the year," and post them on your bulletin board. Following through on promises is key.

ASSEMBLING A PROPOSAL OR LETTER OF INQUIRY

Although calls, meetings, and tours can spark a funder's interest, communicate your values and style, and give you the opportunity to find out about your prospect's goals, 99 percent of the time you still can't get a grant without making a formal request in writing. You will need to create a letter of inquiry, a full proposal, or both, for each grant request.

This is the job so much feared by the average grant seeker, but it will be relatively easy for you after all the learning, matching, and inviting you've already done. Most of your work will be bringing together information you already have saved in your file cabinet and on your computer. Then you will have the relatively simple task of filling in small holes, tailoring the presentation to your particular funder, and smoothing it all into a readable story. Unlike the average grant seeker, you can send your proposal out at least a week ahead of time. You don't need to waste money or time on overnight or hand delivery.

Letters of Inquiry Versus Full Proposals

Sometimes funders request a letter of inquiry (LOI) prior to accepting an unsolicited full proposal. A letter of inquiry is simply a letter that summarizes your intended grant request. LOIs are limited in length (usually two or three pages) and usually do not contain all of the attachments (budgets, boards lists, and so on) that are part of full proposals. LOIs are used by funders to make an initial screening of grant applicants without investing the time and energy necessary to thoroughly consider a full proposal.

From a letter of inquiry a funder can quickly tell if a potential grantee fits basic guidelines such as geographic constraints or their categories of funding (for example, K–12 education). This allows them to steer grant seekers away from working on ill-advised proposals. As a systematic grant seeker you don't need to be afraid of LOIs because you target your efforts to the kind of funders with whom you will have a better-than-average chance of surviving the initial screening.

With LOIs you usually get an answer quickly—perhaps in a few weeks or months as opposed to a year. The answer will be one of three kinds: (1) an outright rejection letter, (2) an invitation to submit a full proposal, or (3) a check. Just as funders can tell from an LOI if you are not eligible, they can sometimes tell that they want to give you a grant and save you the bother of submitting more materials.

The fact that grants can be won with no more than an LOI means you should view the LOI seriously as a brief, focused proposal. We advise against sending a general letter of interest, that is, one that does not state a specific program and grant amount. The similarity of LOIs to full-length grant proposals is especially obvious when the funder provides guidelines for the LOI. The funder might say, for example, "Grant applicants are asked to write a one- or two-page preproposal letter to the Foundation, describing the basic problem to be addressed and the plan for solving the problem. This letter should briefly explain the project objectives, operational procedures, time schedules, and personnel and financial resources available and needed."[1]

If you need to write an LOI to your prospect, follow the directions that follow for writing a full proposal, with appropriate adjustments for the short format of the LOI. Follow the funder's guidelines but anticipate that the LOI format will make work easier for you. You'll be able to skip a lot of steps; for example, you may not need to submit a line item budget.

The challenge will come in being both concise and compelling. You will need to convince the funder that you are worth another, more in-depth look, based solely on your two to three pages of text. Anything absolutely critical or especially persuasive (such as a special line in your budget or a name of an important board member) will need to be mentioned in the text of the letter itself unless the LOI guidelines request attachments.

Parts of a Grant Proposal

There are five parts to a typical grant proposal: a cover sheet, attachments, the narrative, the project budget, and a cover letter.

Often foundations request a *cover sheet* or other means for you to provide basic identifying information about your organization such as contacts, signatures, and so on. There are *attachments* you can or must provide, such as your 501(c)(3) letter. The largest piece of the proposal is often the *narrative,* in which you make the case for funding your program. You'll see narratives required in a variety of forms, but often a funder provides a list of questions you need to answer or topics you need to address. You might have to address these questions or topics on a form the funder provides, or you might be able to use a free-form essay or letter. Usually you must provide a *budget* for your project. Finally, there is a fifth piece of a proposal package. Few funders actually require it, and it isn't technically a part of your proposal, but you will want to add a *cover letter.*

With your deadline card serving as an ever-vigilant reminder on the wall, start working on your proposal by orienting yourself to the materials you need:

➜ Scan the funder's application guidelines once again. This gives you another chance to think about your common goals and the match you're proposing.

➜ Create or obtain a checklist of all the things you need to include in the proposal.

Sometimes a checklist will be provided in the application guidelines. If it is not, you should make one yourself as you scan them. You can use the Proposal Assembly Form (Exhibit A.4) to check for commonly required elements. Having a checklist will ensure you don't miss anything and will give you a sense of security and accomplishment as you move through its items.

Attachments. We like to start work on a proposal by gathering the attachments. This is easy, gives you a nice sense of accomplishment early in the process, and protects you from running around late in the game if it turns out you are missing an attachment you need. So before you work on anything else, do this:

➔ Identify on your checklist all the attachments you have ready to use just as they are, such as your 501(c)(3) letter and audit, and gather them together. These documents should be sitting already prepared in your "Organization and Program" files.

Unless the funder stipulates no extra attachments, always include the organizational resume you created earlier and a relevant program resume, if there is one.

The Budget. Even though the budget usually gets attached at the end of a proposal, we're not surprised when we hear some foundation staff say it is the first thing they read. Here you are forced to state your request in bald numbers, providing the grant maker with a black-and-white snapshot of what your request is really for. The budget establishes your credibility and knowledge of your subject and program. Just as important, it establishes your knowledge of the funder's guidelines and practices. For example, you will provide the funder with an easy opportunity to disqualify you if you ask for a grant far beyond the foundation's giving range. So we recommend that you create the project budget with care, before writing anything.

You already know the basic budget facts and needs of the project for which you are raising money. Your project itself does not change based on the current application. However, for several reasons you will need to make a special edition of the project budget for each grant proposal you are writing. Some funders ask for specific formats or budget categories, which may not be included in the budget you have. Others do not allow you to count certain kinds of expenses (such as existing staff) toward the budget in your request. Finally, if you are actively fundraising for the project, putting together money from different sources, lines in the revenue category may change with some frequency. So do this:

➔ Create a special version of your program budget for your current grant proposal, using the guidelines we discuss next.

The budget you prepare should tell the same story as the narrative you write. It should show where the project money will come from and where it will go, and it should suggest what your program's and organization's priorities are. Any serious mismatch between the narrative and the budget—for example, an emphasis on volunteers in your narrative with little or no projected expense on volunteer recruitment or support—could cast serious doubt on your proposal.

Keep the content and format simple, unless the funder's guidelines direct you to use a specific format. Very few funders require more than a basic project budget, and making it more complex only opens you up for math errors and other budget red flags. For example, errors often occur when grant seekers add a column indicating which pieces of their budgets they are asking various funders to pay for. This calculation can get complicated, and unless the funder requires it of you (which most don't), you should clear your budgets of this kind of added work and detail. Write the budget as a simple layout of revenue and expenses, with revenue at the top and expenses below, as we have done in Exhibit 9.1.

Revenue and expenses should match (it's a perfect world in a grant proposal). In the revenue section put the name of the funder to whom you are applying and the grant amount you are seeking on the very first line. This demonstrates how the funder fits as a crucial part of the overall funding plan for your project and shows how much of the total project you are asking them to fund. Also include your other revenue sources; you know funders want to see that you have others on board.

→ Double check your numbers and your math.

→ Print your budget and place it appropriately, along with the attachments you've gathered.

Because you will have to make budgets often, it will pay to save a budget template in your house style on your computer, using a spreadsheet program like Microsoft Excel. Remember to double check your formula definitions whenever you alter the template (for example, by adding new expense or income categories).

The Free-Form Narrative. The narrative is just one more piece of the proposal. With your preparation, writing it will not be the dreaded job it is for many grant seekers. Every proposal narrative is similar in that it contains the answers to a series of questions about your project and organization. Just as you did in your research notes in Chapter Four, you should try to answer each question with a few clear and compelling sentences or paragraphs. But this time you'll strive to make those sentences and paragraphs flow together into a logical and engaging story.

Exhibit 9.1. Sample Project Budget

Port City Partnership for the Arts
Project 21C Annual Budget for 2001

REVENUES:

Thurston Family Foundation	$15,000	
Foundation A	100,000	
Foundation B	25,000	
Corporate Sponsorship	10,000	
Participants	45,000	*6 times 750 participants × $10*
Participating Member Arts Organizations	80,000	
TOTAL REVENUES		$275,000

EXPENSES

Project coordinator (including benefits)	$47,000	
25% of executive director's time (+ benefits)	22,500	
25% of development director's time (+ benefits)	13,500	
Subsidized arts tickets for 750 participants	67,500	*6 times 750 participants × $15*
Educational mailings	22,500	*6 times 750 participants × $5*
Post-event gatherings	30,000	*3 times 500 participants × $20*
Marketing	44,765	
Meeting expenses w/partner organizations	1,000	
Additional postage	1,200	
Phones	960	
Web site maintenance	2,500	
Transportation	1,575	
Carry over to year two	20,000	
TOTAL EXPENSES		$275,000

Thinking of the narrative as answers to a list of questions is very helpful for two reasons. First, the list of questions can give your writing a strong structure. Second, questions provide great hints for ways to begin narrative sections. If the question is, "How many people will your program serve?" the most obvious and direct way to begin a paragraph in response would be something like, "This program will serve more than two hundred people. Half will be. . . . " These "answer paragraphs" can then be tied together and edited to create a seamless whole, whether or not the questions that inspired them remain on the page. We'll give an example of how this works shortly.

You get the list of questions you will use, in one way or another, from the funder's guidelines. Sometimes guidelines are literally a list of questions. For example, the grant application may be a form you need to fill out or a list of inquiries you are required to address *in order*. This provides a strong structure for your writing, whether you like it or not.

In other cases, such as when a funder asks you to address certain issues in a free-form narrative, or when the funder's guidelines are vague ("Send a letter proposal"), then the funder's inquiries to you are implied. To make progress writing this looser kind of narrative, you can create your own list of questions to outline the text, such as the list we use in the following example, which is designed to show the question-and-answer method of narrative writing in action.

Below you'll find a series of questions (which come from Exhibit A.5 in Resource A). Beneath each question, we'll show you text that begins to answer the question. To see the full text of each answer, and see how it all flows together into a seamless whole, read the narrative of the complete sample grant in Resource B.

1. What is our specific grant request (the amount and for what project)?

Port City Partnership for the Arts respectfully requests a grant of $50,000 from the Thurston Family Foundation. . . .

2. Who *is* our organization? What are its mission and brief history? Whom should the funder contact, and what is that person's phone number, mailing address, fax, and e-mail?

As a Williams Art Foundation program officer, Mary Ryan heard repeatedly from applicants on two points: they needed to continually grow their audiences and reach out to new people, but they also needed to minimize their overhead expenses. In 1990 Ryan left her post at the Williams Foundation to establish the Port City Partnership for the Arts to address these concerns. . . .

3. What is the community need that our organization, and specifically our project, addresses? What statistics and stories can we use to substantiate that need?

Although they have seen hours and hours of television, over a quarter of all Port City elementary school students have never seen a live play. . . .

4. How does our proposed project address the need? What methods will we use? How many people will we serve or involve?

Project 21C will develop the next generation of art supporters and patrons in Port City by engaging young people new to arts attendance in a low-cost, year-long program of arts education, events, performances, and social interaction. . . .

5. What are our measurable project goals or outcomes?

Our goal is to create new interest in the arts among a young and vital segment of our population. We project that by the end of the first operating year. . . .

6. What is our timeline and work plan? Have we included everything from planning to evaluation?

November 2001, Identify participants. . . .

7. Who are the key volunteers and staff on this project, and what are their qualifications? How much of their time will be spent on this particular project?

Project 21C was created and is driven by a twelve-member volunteer Leadership Team, headed by Wendy Branch. Wendy is. . . .

8. What is our projected cost and what are our sources of revenue? How will the project be sustained after the grant period, if applicable? (You can refer to an attached budget in this section.)

The first-year cost for Project 21C will be $275,000; a project budget is attached as per your request. A large portion of this budget is for. . . .

9. What other organizations in the community are providing similar programs or projects? How is ours different? How do we work together with the other providers?

In Port City, PCPA is a unique organization. In fact, within our five-state region, we know of only one other. . . .

10. Why is ours the right organization to launch this program, buy this item, or whatever it is we are proposing?

Our eight years of experience in a field we essentially created makes us the one and only organization with the experience, mission, and existing partnerships to successfully carry out this program. . . .

11. How will our program be evaluated, how often, and by whom? What will the evaluation process do for the program—will it help us adjust the program, replicate it in other cities, or plan in other ways?

It is crucial that a new program make a real difference for people, and the PCPA has three levels of internal review. . . .

12. Who and how many will benefit?

A vital and active arts community is crucial to any healthy city. According to the Research in The Arts institute (RITA), participation in the arts increases self-esteem, problem-solving skills, and imagination at all ages, thereby benefiting. . . .

13. Why are we approaching this funder at this time?

The Thurston Family Foundation has been and continues to be a crucial supporter of Port City's cultural community. . . .

14. How can we best thank the funder for their generosity and consideration?

Thank you for your focus on the arts, and thank you for your consideration of this request. . . .

15. What attachments will we be including?

Organizational Resume, Project Summary Sheet, Board List. . . .

These questions should seem familiar because they are almost exactly the same ones you asked your CEO and program director in Step One, when you invested time in learning about your organization and program. Rather than struggling to simply meet the requirements of the proposal, you'll be able to spend your time on expressing your case in a concise and compelling way.

At this point you may want to create a folder on your computer called "Proposal Pieces" to save the answers to several of these questions, each as an individual document. You will be using the same or similar text over and over, and if you save answers you are happy with, you'll be able to drop them into future proposals and forms quickly. Then you can alter them slightly to suit the overall proposal on which you're working, saving you time while still avoiding the impression of a boilerplate proposal.

Usually you'll end up with a few unanswered questions or unfulfilled details, perhaps in the area of "measurable goals" or "evaluation." You might need to return to the program staff with a quick call or e-mail for the pieces of information that you're lacking.

When you're done answering questions, you need to link and edit your paragraphs until they form a seamless story. We've done this in the sample grant proposal in Resource B. Even though the sample grant narrative follows the outline of our fifteen questions very closely, it still reads fairly naturally and logically. We think that if you were the grant maker, you'd consider funding our imaginary grant request. But even if not, you'd have a positive impression of our credibility and effectiveness, which could serve us well the next time we contact you.

The Funder-Structured Narrative. Sometimes the funder asks for the narrative on a paper form of their design, or on a computer form, or as a list of inquiries that you must respond to in a certain order. In these cases the structure of the narrative is already defined for you, but otherwise you go through the same process we described for the free-form narrative. You answer questions and strive to make those answers form a cohesive whole with a beginning, middle, and end.

Occasionally the defined structure is an awkward one that is not particularly compatible with the goal of telling a cohesive story with a beginning, middle, and end. For example, the first question on the funder's list might be, "How will you evaluate your program?" This is hard to answer before you've described the program. (We casually refer to the worst of these structures as "cubist grants.") In these cases you don't have much choice but to do the best you can. One trick you might use is this: even though you must always answer the funder's question, you may be able to slip in additional information as you answer it. For example, if the first question is about evaluation, you might write, "As an innovative and scientific drug treatment program, we have a rigorous protocol for evaluation. . . ."

Proposals that you must execute on paper or computer forms provide some additional logistical hassles. With paper forms, often the easiest thing to do is to recreate them using your word processing program. (Very few funders require that you type on their original form.)

When you are recreating a form, imitate the funder's layout and fonts as closely as possible without taking hours to match them perfectly. Your goals are to respect the amount of space given to you and make your proposal easy to compare with all the others the funder will receive. Resist the temptation to add space for yourself. The funder made the form for a reason; if you deviate from it too much, you're probably making extra work for the funder's staff and possibly disqualifying yourself. Once you've recreated a form but before you fill it in, save a blank version on your computer in the appropriate funder's folder. That way you'll save time if you apply to this funder again next year.

As of this writing, grant applications on interactive computer forms (those you can fill in on your computer without scanning or recreating them) are relatively rare. Most that exist currently are Web-based forms that you fill in and e-mail to the funder directly from a Web site. These are quick to submit but give you less control over presentation. If you use them, don't let the ease or informality of the process make your work sloppy. You should prepare your answers carefully before sending off the final version.

→ If you haven't started already, now is the time to draw on the methods just described and find or generate a list of questions that will outline your grant proposal's narrative.

→ Using our question-and-answer method, write a first draft of your narrative. You will edit it later, so it doesn't have to be absolutely perfect, but all the content should be there.

→ At this point you may also need to compose any attachments that are required but that you did not have prepared in your files. For example, a funder might request a page of top donors' names.

Cover Sheet and Cover Letter. We advise leaving the cover sheet until after the bulk of the proposal is written. The cover sheet is often a summary of the whole proposal, and when you have the whole proposal in front of you, it will be easier to summarize it properly. Remember that a cover sheet is not the same as a cover letter; a cover sheet is part of a proposal, often required by the funder; a cover letter is a courteous note that goes on top of your proposal and indicates that your proposal is enclosed in the envelope.

→ Fill in the funder's cover sheet. Some funders require that you type on their form. Otherwise, you may recreate their form on your computer.

→ If the funder does not require a cover sheet, you don't need to make one. Your clearly written narrative and copies of your organization and program resumes will tell them all they need to know.

→ Place any required cover sheet on top of your narrative, budget, and attachments.

Note any signatures that are required, and plan to meet up with the appropriate people, such as your board president, to collect these before the proposal deadline. Write a one-page cover letter, referencing any conversations or meetings you've had with the funder, your exact request, and one key point. Keep it brief and professional. Place the cover letter on top of everything else, and the first draft of your proposal is finished!

EDITING THE PROPOSAL

Now that you have a living, breathing draft of a proposal, you should get away from it for a few days or at least a few hours. Then you will want to revisit it with a fresh mind, getting edits and reactions from two parties: yourself and those who are responsible for the project you are trying to fund, such as the program staff. The latter review is essential to grant seeking with integrity.

Your Colleagues' Review

You might have a fantastic grant approach and proposal, practically guaranteed to earn your agency all the money it could want. But before you send it off, it is essential that you get the insight and approval from the people who will be responsible for executing the project, such as the program staff. They need to check your facts and confirm exactly what will be expected of them if they get the money. They need to enter the grant deal with every expectation they can fulfill their side of it. As the grant seeker you need to be careful here. The editing process is a stage where your efficient five-step grant-seeking system can bog down for several reasons, chiefly because it is out of your direct control and usually involves the input of very busy people. The people reviewing your draft may not know as much about the funder or the grant-seeking process as you. They also might believe it's their duty as "editors" to make big changes to your carefully constructed proposal.

Before you dive into this process and send your proposal to a few key people for their important review, you will need to decide who these people should be and consider the needs that different parties have in the process. As the grant seeker you need speed and predictability so you'll meet your deadline. Your internal reviewers need ample opportunity to read and edit, as well as the confidence that any substantial comments they make will be heard. Consider these factors and then do the following:

→ Decide on one or two key people to ask to edit your proposal. These will probably include one program person and your CEO. This choice doesn't need to be set in stone. Later in the book we'll walk you through defining an official editing process. But for now just choose one or two people for this first time through the grant cycle.

→ Give your draft proposal (stamped DRAFT) only to these relevant internal reviewers. Include a memo or cover note asking them to proof or edit the proposal. Include a deadline for returning the material to you prominently on the first page of the draft.

The memo and the deadline may seem formal but are important, especially if it is the first time you and your internal reviewers are going through an editing process. The memo can set a couple of ground rules for them. For example, you can remind them that they are not approving a new program idea. We hope that was done well before the idea got to the proposal stage. They are simply *proofing this proposal.* They need to make changes only if something is inaccurate; they don't need to worry about writing style. This should help make the task less onerous. The response deadline is key, because it prompts you to remind people if they don't respond. You may also tell reviewers that if they do not respond, they may be exempted from the editing process by the CEO if a funder's deadline is near. You can decide whether this step is necessary, given your organization and the particular deadline on which you're working.

Finally, the memo gives you a chance to thank people for working on this proposal with you. They'll see that your grant-seeking work is progressing and that the time they've invested with you was well spent.

→ Keep records of the deadlines you give your internal reviewers. In the future when you are working on multiple proposals, this will become important.

Your Own Review

Once you have at least a few hours' distance from your first draft, sit down at a clean table with it. As you read it, try to think about it from the point of view of the foundation staff person or trustee who will receive it.

General Presentation. Your readers might have a stack of dozens of proposals in front of them. You want to make your proposal the first one they pick up. It should look inviting and easy to read. There should be a significant amount of white space on the page, in margins and other places, not just forbidding black blocks of text. Elements like headers, footers, page numbers, and section headings can help guide the reader.

You should follow the funder's instructions in both letter and spirit. The foundation invented its guidelines for a reason, and if you ignore them you can seem ignorant or disrespectful. If a funder asks for three pages, give three regular pages. Don't crunch margins beyond 0.5 inches or use type below 11 point. (In fact, we start with 1-inch margins and 12- or 12.5-point type as our ideal.) And don't ever go beyond the pages allowed or add attachments that a funder stipulates against in its guidelines (such as videos or extra support letters). Even if a funder doesn't stipulate page limits, there is probably something wrong if your narrative is longer than ten pages (many government and scientific proposals excepted). Check to be sure you haven't given too much detail or gotten off track.

The length of your narrative is essential to communicating your message effectively. Eliminate unnecessary detail, which can be wearying for the reader. The person reading the proposal does not usually need to know things like the number of shifts on your homeless shelter's second floor. We use a "toaster guideline": if you were buying a toaster, you would need information about each toaster's features and benefits in order to choose the one you prefer, but you would not need to know the technicalities of how the toaster works inside. If you feel a narrative longer than eight pages is really merited, consider including a table of contents.

Beyond an attractive look and an appropriate level of detail, the general consistency of your work can make the proposal easier to comprehend and increase your underlying message of confidence and capability. Check for logical segues between different sections of the narrative, and double check that the narrative and the budget tell the same story.

Argument and Style. Another thing that can make your proposal easier to read is a clear and cogent argument. If readers must struggle just to understand your project, then they're going to have trouble appreciating its fantastic benefits. A grant proposal is no place for poetic abstraction. The writing should guide the reader along a logical through-line (for example, from need to solution to details).

Striving for clarity and logic doesn't mean you need to be boring. When you read your draft with a fresh mind, you should feel interest and want to read to the end. You may even get excited about the project (a good sign). If you're not excited or, worse yet, if you're bored, the funder probably will feel the same way. Go back and work on sustaining the reader's interest with stories, direct statements of your organization's compelling vision, and clear, crisp language that is free of jargon.

Strike a balance between statistics and anecdotes, between big ideas and program specifics. Change overly bureaucratic or impersonal language. For example, change the word *clients* to *people* or *families;* ensure that the writing is smart yet easy to read.

We won't go further into the fine points of writing style in grant proposals because we think using a steady, intelligent approach and making the right matches is more important than eloquence. If you want more tips on the writing of grant proposal narratives, see one of our favorite books: *Grassroots Grants: An Activist's Guide to Proposal Writing* by Andy Robinson.[2]

Another Review

If you have a willing test subject, a good practice is to run your draft proposal by someone who is not involved with your nonprofit. Outside readers such as family members or friends can be a great gauge as to whether your proposal is clear and understandable to the uninitiated.

The Second Draft

When you've made notes on the draft and collected all the comments from your reviewers, it's time to bring them all together.

→ Keep all those comments in mind as you edit and smooth the first draft of your grant proposal into a polished second draft.

→ Give the second draft to your CEO with a deadline for his or her final review.

→ Create the third and final draft.

→ Double check that the proposal is assembled properly.

At this point there are some common mistakes to avoid, so use your Proposal Assembly Form or other checklist and make sure to do things like these:

→ Have the appropriate people sign any cover letters and forms.

→ Make the exact number of copies the funder asks for.

→ Make sure the paper is bound, hole-punched, or assembled according to the funder's instructions.

If there are no instructions for printing and presentation, use a standard method. We like to use one-side printed, white paper that is not hole-punched or bound but held together with a binder clip. This makes it easy for foundation staff to photocopy, which many will need to do, and it keeps the proposal from looking fussy or expensive.

CONGRATULATIONS

Your proposal is now ready to go to the funder. Although constructing a proposal is definitely a significant piece of labor, we doubt it was the nightmare for you that it is for other, less prepared grant seekers.

Your next steps depend on your situation. You will certainly want to mail out your grant proposal, which marks the beginning of Step Four of the grant-seeking cycle. We'll do that in Chapter Eleven. You can skip there now if you'd like. You may also be pursuing or preparing for meetings or site visits with your funder or working to take advantage of other kinds of personal relationships. Although these activities could happen before or after you mail out your grant proposal, conceptually those subjects are part of Step Three—your invitation to the funder. We'll cover them next in Chapter Ten.

Guide Relationships, Meetings, and Tours

Early in our grant-seeking careers we attended a workshop in which the expert presenter told us, "If you don't get a meeting first, you're not going to get a donation." He believed that those of us who were told to "send it in writing" were doomed. You may have received some similar foreboding advice. Our experience, as we noted in Chapter Nine, has not borne this out. We have received dozens of grants of all sizes with and without meetings and tours. Securing any one meeting won't make or break your grants effort.

You've invested time in finding a good match. Now your goal should be to establish a business relationship rather than to arrange any one meeting. The relationship should be based on mutual esteem and proof of good work and integrity. If you really believe your funders are your colleagues rather than your superiors, you should be able to adopt the right form of communication, based on the substance of what you have to relate and your respect for the funder's time. Phone calls, meetings, site visits, proposals, letters, and so on all have their place in your invitations to funders.

In this chapter we'll cover some of the more personal kinds of communications you can make and the considerable value they can have. After discussing various kinds of business relationships that can be involved in and fruitful for your grant-seeking work, we'll cover conducting the two most common types of face-to-face encounters: (1) a meeting at the funder's office and (2) a funder's visit to your site (or some other location). We can't give you a recipe for exactly what to say and when to say it, but we can give you some of the principles of cultivating grant-seeking relationships with a positive attitude.

BUSINESS RELATIONSHIPS

Certainly there are times when very personal relationships make grants and other kinds of donations happen. Someone on your board might know someone who is wealthy or influential; a phone call is made, and the deal is arranged. Fundraising consultant and author Terry Axelrod calls this particular brand of relationship fundraising "strong-arming-thy-Rolodex" and writes that when a friend plied this kind of fundraising on her, she at first gave in. But when the friend left the board of the organization in question, Axelrod stopped donating. Why? "Because they never took the time to win me over directly, because they never gave me the opportunity to fall in love with them directly, I stopped giving to them as soon as I felt I could," she writes.[1]

In her example the fundraising was based entirely on a personal relationship and had no stability or long-term promise for the organization. To keep this from happening to your organization the next time your board changes composition, you need to cultivate business relationships with funders that are based on their authentic interests and your common goals. To do that you *don't* need to impress people with your suit, just with your programs. You *don't* need to take everyone in town to lunch or hand out your business cards like you're dealing a poker hand at every Rotary breakfast you attend. You do need to contact grant makers with thoughtful questions, information, and invitations; when appropriate, have other staff and board members do the same.

This less personal attitude toward relationships shows your respect for grant makers. Most of the funding staff and trustees we've met strive to be objective and would be insulted by the implication that someone's closeness to them or the cloying phone calls and letters they receive would affect their funding decisions. However, such a colleague would never be insulted by meaningful communications about your organization and its programs—be they facts and figures, questions, or endorsements.

Board-to-Board Relationships and Communications

It's not uncommon for there to be relationships among a funder's trustees and your board members. As these people are often active or prominent figures in your community, some individuals may already know one another. In fact, your board may have been carefully assembled just for its community networking potential. As the grant seeker for your organization, your job is to find out about these relationships and tap them judiciously:

→ Periodically provide your board with a list of trustees from foundations you have recently applied to or plan to apply to in the near future. Request that the board circle the names of people they know well enough to write or call and return the list to you.

If you discover a relationship, consider asking your board member to call or write to the foundation trustee in question. If you have already sent a proposal, the board member can endorse it. If not, he or she can send a personal note along with a complete copy of your proposal when you send the original proposal itself through the foundation's proper channels.

The idea behind such an endorsement or note is to demonstrate the high level of volunteer commitment and leadership associated with your program. This should be a real commitment because your board member may be questioned personally about your program and will need to speak accurately and passionately about it. We advise that your board member should have already demonstrated support for the program, for example, by volunteering for it or making significant personal contributions to it. In addition, you should never overstate a relationship between your board member and a grant maker's trustee. An exaggeration here will be exposed if the trustee reads the proposal.

It's important to remember that the foundation trustee who receives a call or letter may not be the only person affected by it. Larger foundations will have staff people who administer grant-making and review and recommend grant proposals. These staff people are your colleagues and potential advocates; you don't want to alienate them by going over their heads with your connection to a trustee. Some grants consultants might advise you to go for your highest possible connection first, but we have seen this backfire more than once when a foundation staff member became upset by this move. Going directly to the highest connection may add an extra, unintended insult if it is perceived to imply that grants can be won on a purely subjective and personal basis.

Certainly you should contact your highest-level connections in the funder's office, but do so in a way that respects staff. Consider notifying any program staff you know at a foundation when any correspondence is sent to his or her trustees, or consider sending all correspondence through the foundation staff.

Besides notes and endorsements there are other ways a board member can show commitment, whether or not the member has an existing relationship with foundation representatives. If a close personal relationship exists with trustees who fund (or could fund) your organization, urge your board members to introduce you to these contacts, involve you and your organization's staff people in meetings, and otherwise help forge a working relationship that will last beyond the person's board tenure. If no such relationships exist, you can educate and encourage your board members about how to build them. Your board members can attend lunches or workshops where foundation trustees speak locally and attend meetings and site visits you set up with funders.

Finally, don't despair if your board is not incredibly well connected. We have seen that small, new grant-seeking efforts can succeed without preexisting relationships. We once launched a grant-seeking effort that raised 10 percent of an organization's funding in one year without a single existing relationship. Our success was built on our program's excellent reputation in the community and our willingness to research funding leads and mail targeted proposals week after week. If you have strong programs and plans and you approach grant seeking with integrity and perseverance, you can create the relationships and earn the respect you need.

Staff-to-Staff Relationships

An important type of connection is the working relationship you develop with a funder's staff members. As we mentioned, they are your colleagues and potential allies. They may be your voice at the table when funding decisions are being made, and you want them to have a positive impression of you and your organization, as well as clear, compelling written information about your programs.

Just like any other business relationships, you can initiate these yourself by making the introductory calls we discussed in Chapter Nine, by asking for informational meetings, and by asking grant makers for their advice as well as their foundations' money. You can earn their respect by bringing them excellent programs to fund and by respecting their knowledge, their time, and their foundations' missions. You can learn more about their perspectives by attending workshops and conferences where they're speaking or attending, talking with them about what they do, and staying informed about grant-making trends and issues.

Once you've gone through the grant-seeking cycle a number of times, this kind of advanced research will become more important and valuable to you, and you'll want to make it a regular part of your work. For the time being you can initiate this kind of communication by arranging a first meeting or tour with the funder you're currently asking for money.

MEETINGS WITH FUNDERS

Meetings with funders have great potential. They are encounters where, if you have a purpose, you can exchange a lot of valuable information in a short time. You can get to know one another and gauge how well your organizations fit with one another. Just as the in-person interview you conducted with your CEO in Chapter Four may have revealed stories, facts, and feelings about your organization that were not printed anywhere, in-person conversations with funders can instill confidence in your organization and communicate more than written documents alone. Jamaal T. Folsom of the Black United Fund of Oregon uses in-person meetings to look for evidence that a potential grantee has strong community networks. He also says, "If a person is organized in their conversations with me, I imagine that may be the way they run their programs." At the same time that a meeting helps a grant maker learn about you, you can learn similar things about a grant maker. You can find out about projects a grant maker is especially proud of funding. You may also learn about the grant maker's level of formality and degree of comfort with your organization.

If a meeting isn't tied to a proposal that already exists, you may be able to float a specific proposal idea and get the funder's reaction to it. However, the meeting format has some limitations. Meetings do not take the place of proposals; the two are not interchangeable. Very rarely will a funder be inclined or empowered to give you a grant based on a meeting, with no formal written request, so you should expect to have to write a letter or proposal eventually.

When you are involved in a meeting with a foundation representative, your role is to coordinate your organization's presentation. You will want to limit the number of people attending this meeting and prepare them to get the most out of it.

Advise your CEO to bring just one person—perhaps two if you know that two or three of the funder's people will be there. You don't want to gang up on a funder, but you do want to provide a useful range of representatives. One staff person and one board volunteer is typical. In some circumstances you will need to attend. Examples of those times would be when you have specific questions about the application process or you want to introduce yourself as the new grant seeker at your organization.

Whether or not you are attending, you should talk with your representatives about the purpose of the meeting. Review the reason for the meeting, the specific things you want to accomplish or find out, and the kind of substantial points you want to make about your programs. Remind your people to take no more than their scheduled time.

➔ As an aid in preparing the people going to the meeting, write up and distribute the short handout we call a Project Summary Form.

The Project Summary Form is shown in Exhibit 10.1 and available as a blank form in Exhibit A.6.

During this meeting your party may need to start out by giving the funder's representatives some context for why they're there. Your party should introduce your organization and program or project. If there is a history with the funder, they may also want to briefly recap your organization's accomplishments using previous grants. Then your party can get to their main purpose. Because they're most likely there to get answers or advice, they should allow the funder to talk. There's no need to interrupt again and again with talking points or sales pitches.

If your party is there with the intention of floating a proposal idea with the funder, they should mention the specific dollar amount they're thinking of requesting. They shouldn't expect to get a funding commitment during the meeting, but they might receive some kind of advice or impression, such as a clue that the amount mentioned is too high or too low or that a funder would be most interested in a certain element of your project. In some cases they may not even get that much; a grant maker may not be able to give specific direction. A funder may quite logically say, "You should ask us for what you need."

Exhibit 10.1. Project Summary Form

Use this form to prepare people in your organization for meetings or site visits with funders.

Name of funder: ___The Lake Foundation___

Site visit on: ___September 10, 2001___ (date and time)

Or meeting on: _____ (date and time)

At: ___the black box theatre___ (location)

Our staff or volunteers who will be attending:

Jeanmarie, Director

Ken, board Member

Funder representatives who will be attending:

Eli Higgins, chair

Purpose or main goal of meeting or visit:

To introduce ourselves to their new chair and show him the new theater space we're sharing with Parallax (a grantee of theirs).

Funder's mission:

To support artists who are forming their own production companies and nonprofit organizations!

A few typical grants they made last year:

$5,000 to The Artists' Zoo, experimental gallery, for 1st major show

$10,000 to Parallax, modern dance group, for first subscription series

$7,500 to Voices, poetry reading series

Their grant range in dollars: __$2,000 to $10,000__

Name of our proposed project: __"7–11"__

Grant amount we've requested: __$8,000__

One-sentence description of our project:

"7–11" is an evening of seven 11-minute plays about gambling, literally or figuratively

Three key points about our project:

1. Walleyed Productions was formed last year by a group of actors, directors, and writers.

2. This is our first ever annual short play festival.

3. $8,000 will pay for marketing and ticket sales, helping us establish business systems for the future.

Check one:

____x____ We have already sent a proposal to this funder.

_____ We can have a proposal to this funder by _____ (date).

After the meeting with the funder, there are several things you should do:

➔ Make sure that your representatives write a thank-you note to the funder, referring to when your proposal will be coming. Courtesies like this are easy and can make a difference.

➔ Write up any notes about the meeting and stick them in the funder's file. If you did not attend the meeting, ask your CEO for a short memo or e-mail on the subject.

➔ If your party received advice about a date to submit a written proposal or agreed to do any other things by certain dates, create appropriate deadline cards and hang them on your bulletin board.

➔ Using your newfound insight into the funder, think about how to adjust your approach in the future.

THE TOUR OR SITE VISIT

If you have a good reason to ask for one, a tour or site visit by your potential funder (where the funder's representatives come to your place) can be a valuable part of your grant request. The site visit has the potential to excite and interest even world-weary foundation staff. Amy Brown, development director for the Oregon Children's Foundation and its early literacy program SMART (Start Making A Reader Today), arranges school tours on which funders observe children reading together with SMART volunteers. The tours "engage them in the passion and emotion of the program," she says. "They see the enthusiasm of the children and the enthusiasm and competency of the volunteers. This is beyond what we can convey on paper."

Like meetings, site visits can come before or after you've sent a written proposal. Sometimes your potential funder will request or require one as part of the normal grants review process. Your goal during a site visit is to give the funder a direct dose of the unique energy, commitment, and mission carried out every day in your office, facility, or space.

To prepare for a site visit, you will want to think about what areas of your place you want to share, what sights and experiences should come first and last, and whom you want to stop and talk with along the way, such as key volunteers or staff people. You don't want to make the tour a tiring one—long or verbally detailed. Nor do you want to overwhelm the funder's representatives with facts that may be more clearly presented in a written proposal. Let your organization and its vibrant activities or special features speak for themselves, and keep speeches by you or your CEO concise. Be sure to leave room in your presentation for your guests to react and ask questions or to give you their ideas.

One of our favorite tours was given by a lieutenant at The Salvation Army in Portland, who had just completed work on his community center with the help of a large grant. We asked the funder to visit to see how things were going before we asked for another donation. One of the elements of the community center was a vintage swimming pool with rare, hand-tiled craftsmanship. We got a tour around the underside of the pool in the basement—a trip that communicated the lieutenant's incredible pride as well as something unique about our site. In addition, it gave us the opportunity to talk about the work the funder's grant paid for and the children and senior citizens who used the pool and benefited from the grant maker's generosity. Another fun tour included a school lunch in a cafeteria for a grant maker who was funding a nutrition program for children.

The idea isn't to create a theatrical marvel but to arrange an authentic experience that will engage people emotionally with your site or program while getting across some basic facts and also giving them an opportunity to speak. For example, a horseback ride might be fun for a (willing) funder of a children's ranch, but if the ride comprises the entire site visit, you won't get to ask for crucial suggestions and advice about your next proposal. You will want to schedule a place and time to sit down and meet after the "tour" portion of the visit. (If you plan to ask people to participate in anything unusual, dirty, or at all strenuous, *ask* them first before you plan your tour.)

Although we recommend that you ask for a site visit only if you have something to show, sometimes a visit will be required by a funder, even if your program is run out of a one-room back office. In this circumstance do what you can to express the passion of your organization. For example, take the funder on a tour outside your office to see the neighborhood in which you make a difference, or invite a volunteer or two to be present with you.

As the visit nears, prepare for it much as you would a meeting. Limit the number of people who will play the role of hosts, and prepare them for the experience with your Project Summary Form. Feel free to remind other staff that a visit is upcoming, but don't over-prepare the building and every person in it. The funder is usually visiting you to find out what your operations are really like. If you "dress up" so much that you seem less than genuine or you hide a real need, it could hurt your chances to get funded.

For example, if you are a grassroots environmental organization but you have everyone wear business suits on the day of a site visit, your office culture may come across as strangely discontinuous with your mission and programs. Or if you are applying for a grant for a new building on the basis that yours is too small but then hide all the extra boxes of supplies that are normally under peoples' desks and in the bathrooms, your need may not be viscerally apparent; you will undermine the whole purpose of the tour.

➜ Following a site visit take the same steps you would take after a meeting, including sending thank-you notes to the grant makers who visited you, making and filing any notes, and creating any relevant deadline cards to keep you on track with your promises.

➜ If the site visit was a great success, write down what was good about it.

The more experienced you become with meetings and site visits, the easier they will be to plan and execute. If you really believe in your organization and its programs, they might even become a joy.

Follow Up with Your Organization and Your Funder

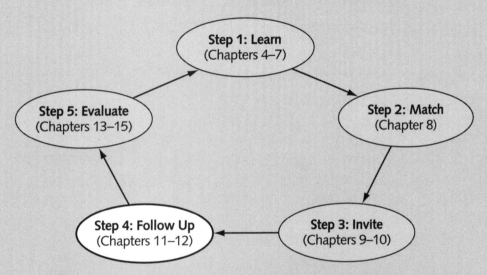

Making an invitation to a prospective funder is not the end of the grant-seeking process. Follow-up is essential, both within your organization and with your funder. Internally, you need to keep people informed about the grants process and involved in it. With the funder you need to respond to the result of your invitation, whether the result is in the form of a check in the mail, an invitation to submit a full proposal, a request for a visit to see your program in action, or a flat-out rejection. You keep the funder engaged, and cultivate a collegial relationship—one worthy of fair deals between equals.

Communicate After Mailing a Proposal

If this book were just about proposal writing, we might have a very short chapter about follow-up at this point. But we don't want to give you the impression that mailing off a proposal is the end of the grant-seeking process. Naturally, once a proposal is in the mail, you should take some pride in your accomplishment and go home early. But when you get back to the office, don't lose sight of two realities. First, simple things you do now can affect your chances to get the money you've asked for. Second, sending off a proposal is the beginning of another set of opportunities for you to build relationships with colleagues, inside and outside your organization—relationships that can pay off with grant funding in the future, regardless of the verdict about your most recent proposal.

In this chapter we'll take you through the process of sending off and tracking your proposals and communicating with four important groups of people: (1) the staff of your prospective funder, who now have your proposal in hand, (2) your organization's staff, (3) your board of directors, and (4) your coworkers in the development office.

FINISHING YOUR WORK WITH A PROPOSAL

When you're sure your proposal is complete, you need to make copies of the whole grant package for your own records. We suggest you do this in a very particular way:

→ Make one copy of the *signed* proposal on *colored* paper, and put it in the "Funder" file for the grant maker you are applying to. If you make copies for other people, you can make them on regular paper.

→ Then put the signed proposal in the mail.

If these procedures seem overly specific, consider a few good reasons for being meticulous at this point. In our experience grant proposals sometimes change significantly throughout the editing process as a concept evolves and internal reviewers make comments. You want to make sure your file copy really is the same document you sent to the funder. It could be damaging to your credibility if a funder called to ask about your request for $15,000 and you were unable to answer questions because your copy said you were asking for $5,000. That's why you should make your file copy at the last minute. Use colored paper for your file copy because it helps identify the proposals you've sent among the growing abundance of papers in your "Funder" files; you'll be thankful for this when you are in a hurry to find your proposal.

The potential information overload in your office makes this a good time to practice two habits of the effective grant seeker: (1) clearing your workspace and (2) limiting what you keep. Be an informed but ruthless tosser.

→ Take some time to recycle all unnecessary grant-related material in your paper and electronic files.

→ File those few items you need to keep, making sure they are each clearly dated with month, day, and year.

You do not need to save notes that led up to writing a proposal because the proposal itself includes all the relevant information you collected and the final versions of any timelines or budgets. Two years from now, no one will need to know that you had a meeting scheduled for noon on Tuesday with the program director. Keep only final proposals, actual correspondence, brief records of meetings with the funder, copies of checks or agreements, and copies of the funder's guidelines and annual reports.

When you date the materials you keep, include the year. Too many times we've rolled up our sleeves to clean out vast grant files that resulted from half a decade of work to find everything marked with dates like "8/23" and "5/6." This kind of confusion makes it hard to determine the recent history of your relationship with the funder and makes it hard to target new proposals effectively.

Finally, perform a ritual signifying that the heavy lifting of going for this grant is over:

→ Take the relevant deadline card down off the wall and put it back in the box for next year. (You can allow yourself to feel smug and satisfied at this point.)

TRACKING YOUR EFFORTS

Now that you have a proposal in the mail, perform a bit of systematic record keeping to track your efforts. In the short term this will remind you of the proposals you have pending. In the long term your tracking data can provide valuable information for targeting future grant proposals.

All you need to track your work is something as simple as our Overall Tracking Form, which is illustrated in Exhibit 11.1 and available as a blank form in Exhibit A.7.

This form gives you the big picture of how your grants program is doing and helps you estimate when you ought to hear about proposals you sent out. Take a moment to do the following:

Exhibit 11.1. Overall Tracking Form

Date of proposal	Funder name	Program or project proposed	Amount of request	Result	Result date
9.1.00	Foster Family Fund	Public education campaign	$8,000	Declined	12.1.00
9.15.00	The Webb Trust for Nature	Wildlife monitoring volunteer project	$20,000	$15,000	11.15.00
10.1.00	J. Wheeler Outdoor Trust	Wildlife monitoring volunteer project	$5,000		
10.10.00	The Lunch Foundation	PSA production	$10,000		

→ Record the proposal you mailed on your own Overall Tracking Form.

→ Place your Overall Tracking Form in your "Grant Tracking" folder, which has been waiting patiently in your file cabinet.

Once you have used this form for a while, you can provide monthly reports to your boss and board, project grant income for the coming year, calculate your grant success rate, and so on. You'll find it very handy when a director or the board wants a report of all the proposals made in a certain period. (For example, this information is often necessary if your organization applies to the United Way.) But another benefit is that you may discover trends in the pattern of grant proposals you've won and lost, giving you some wisdom about what to apply for next. You can do all these things using just six simple columns of information.

Resist the temptation to plunge into using a computer program to track grants. Unlike a computer program, our paper form is understandable and accessible to just about anyone. Moreover, learning or creating a computer database can be a huge distraction that gets you no closer to winning grants. We've had success tracking our grants using simple sheets of paper like the one shown in Exhibit 11.1 and have devoted the time we saved to writing more and better proposals. We allow that in a few situations a computer program would really help—perhaps if you have more than a few dozen grants in process at once or you manage several grant seekers at different sites. If you do need such a system, it will become obvious soon enough. In the meantime we want you to use the paper system—at least for the time you use this book to guide your grant-seeking efforts.

COMMUNICATING WITH YOUR PROSPECTIVE FUNDER

Now that your proposal is in your prospective funder's hands, you may have some opportunities to build your relationship further. You do want to stay on the funder's radar screen and provide any interesting news or invitations that might affect the funding decision, but you don't want to be annoying. The way to strike the right balance is to remember that you're the funder's colleague, not the funder's supplicant. Communicate when there is something of substance to discuss.

For example, write to your prospect if you receive an important piece of funding for your project from some other source. This demonstrates that other funders take your project seriously and that the prospect's funding could be the last piece needed. You can use an opportunity like this to reiterate an especially impressive part of your proposal. And now may be the time to ask for a meeting or site visit; the funder's policies may have prohibited one before. (See Chapter Ten for more information about meetings and visits.) Although you never want to nag a funder for a decision, if it's been a very long time since you mailed your proposal (perhaps more than six months), it's appropriate to check on its status.

COMMUNICATING WITH KEY PEOPLE

Beyond maintaining your link with your funder colleagues, you should make a significant effort to communicate within your organization about your grant-seeking work. In purely practical terms other people will be handling grant-related communications and materials such as funder inquiries and checks in the mail. Moreover, when your coworkers are informed about your work, together you may be able to use your combined creativity and connections to enhance all your organization's fundraising.

Your Organization's Staff

Certain people in your office—either paid staff or volunteers—are most likely to have contact with a funder while your proposal is pending. This includes key people listed on your proposal, such as your CEO and board members, and usually extends to people who answer your organization's phone, people who open the mail, and others in similar positions. You need to get these people in the loop.

➜ List all the people whose names and phone numbers appear in proposals you've recently sent out, writing them in here:

☞ _____

➜ List any other people who would be primarily responsible for executing the programs for which you are seeking grants:

☞ _____

➜ List any other people who might have contact with a funder in person, through the phone, mail, or otherwise (for example, mail room staff):

☞ _____

→ Talk to each of these people, educating them about the possibility that funders may call or visit and that these calls should be referred to particular people (the "key contacts" described later).

→ Periodically—perhaps once a month or once a quarter—send each of these people a copy of your Overall Tracking Form so the names of your current and potential funders will be fresh in their minds.

→ You may also want to send copies of your Overall Tracking Form to anyone else who has been involved in your grant-seeking work so far, so they feel a sense of progress and participation.

A few of the people you've listed should be truly qualified to answer detailed inquiries about the grant proposal. These are the funder's "key contacts" at your organization. This group nearly always includes the CEO and your proposal's program director and may extend to important leadership-level volunteers (such as your organization's founder who still volunteers with you or your board president).

→ Identify the key contacts in your organization, and write their names in here:

 _____

These people need to know how to find grant proposals in case funders call when you are not in. Even though you may have provided them with their own copies, it's likely that by now the copies will have been lost or recycled. Or your CEO might not want a copy of every proposal you send out but will need to find the right one when the time comes. The bottom line is that you should not be the only person in your office who knows where things are.

→ Make sure the "key contacts" know about your grants management system and how things are filed, particularly how to find a grant proposal in the "Funder" files.

A quick tour of your area during a management meeting, repeated every few months, is an easy way to accomplish this.

Your Board of Directors

You need to make a consistent effort to keep the board informed of your grant-seeking work. Besides the important relationships this communication might uncover, occasionally a foundation trustee or staff person will call one of your board members. That's why they request board phone numbers in your proposals.

→ Set aside time each month or quarter to create a short "grants report" for the board.

Aim to make this report no more than one page because board members receive a lot of reading material. The page should include a brief list of pending grant applications, described with only essential details: the funder, project name, amount requested, and what staff member at your organization to contact for more information. Plan to write this report so it can be sent out with any packets or other materials the board will get before each meeting. Usually someone in development or in the CEO's office handles board packets and can let you know when to schedule this into your work week.

If you've received any grants recently, don't neglect to include news about those, along with your thanks to any board members who assisted you in the process. The recognition just might inspire others to brainstorm about foundation contacts they have.

Your Development Coworkers

Your organization should have other development efforts going on at the same time you're seeking grants. If your organization is big enough to have other development staff specializing in areas like individual giving and benefit events, communication within your office has potential for a kind of synergy that could really pay off.

On a mundane level everyone in the office has an interest in making sure that funders—be they individuals or foundations—are recorded and acknowledged properly. You may need to watch out for a kind of foul-up we have observed at nonprofits of all sizes: grant checks arrive in the mail and are incorrectly recorded and acknowledged as individual gifts. This leaves you, the grant seeker, unaware that you have won a grant and your funder potentially offended or confused, having received the kind of receipt or thank-you letter normally sent to individuals. Circulating your Overall Tracking Form can help avoid these kinds of mix-ups and ensure proper recognition and follow-up for your foundation donors.

Circulating your tracking form is also an example of the kind of communication that could lead to a really coordinated and synergistic effort among the different parts of your development office. For example, your organization might have received a grant from a local foundation whose trustees include local business owners who are also significant personal donors to community charities. Those business owners might then become prospects for major individual and planned gifts because they've demonstrated an interest in your organization's work. Communication like this could go all ways, and when it is conducted with respect and intelligence, it could help everyone work toward their common dreams.

A more common scenario occurs when you don't communicate with your coworkers. A donor who is also a business owner and a trustee of a local foundation might receive several kinds of appeals from your organization's various development officers. Examples might be an annual appeal letter from individual giving, a capital campaign approach from major giving, a sponsorship approach from event management, and a grant proposal from you. Instead of communicating a strong case for funding, the collective message you might be sending is one of disorganization and carelessness.

When each development department is motivated by an effort to reach its own financial goals, cross-pollination and communication is difficult. But it's in your best interest to make sure that miscommunication doesn't happen. If you work with other fundraisers and you don't know much about their work, ask them. You can lead the way to cooperation by making it part of your system to share your work with your colleagues. (If you work alone, you can take a minute to catch your breath and appreciate this one area of work that's *easier* for you.)

CONGRATULATIONS

You have just started to use a powerful tool that goes unused by too many grant seekers: communication after a proposal is mailed but before a funding decision is made. Communication within your organization can prevent problems and create positive synergy. Keeping in touch with a prospective funder, when done judiciously, can set your organization apart from the others in that grant maker's stack. As an effective grant seeker, you will make these kinds of communication a regular part of your five-step grant-seeking cycle.

Follow Up After a Funding Decision

Finally the big day comes. You receive a response from a funder in the mail. Regardless of the verdict in the envelope, your grant-seeking effort is far from over. You're conducting a steady, systematic effort, and you will soon have a number of different grant requests in different stages of development. This one envelope won't make or break you. No matter what it contains, you're ready to use it to keep building your working relationship with the funder.

IF YOU GOT REJECTED

Even the worthiest programs get rejected. You could have done everything right and still have been turned down. But there are other sources of funding out there, and your system will find them. In the meantime begin to learn what you can from the experience:

→ *Do* mark the result down on your Overall Grant Tracking Form.

→ *Don't* obsess about it or get bitter. It's not personal.

→ *Don't* despair. You're not going to get every grant you apply for.

→ *Do* continue to strengthen your relationship with the funder. *In particular,* if it seems appropriate and you can do so in a professional manner, try to find out why your organization didn't get funded.

→ *Don't* plead, argue, whine, threaten, or try to get the foundation staff to change the funding decision.

→ Calling in the wake of a rejection may seem especially difficult. You may want to wait a few days so you can maintain your professional composure. Even then you often won't be able to find out why you were rejected or even get through to the right person. But if you can get through, you may learn some invaluable information that could improve your future grant seeking.

If you are unsure how to make your first approach after a rejection, remember you are a partner of the funder, not a supplicant. Approach the funder's staff with courtesy and respect, not slobbering praise, sadness, disbelief, or anger. You are a professional colleague with compatible purposes, and you want to get all the advice you can about how best to fund your programs. If you really believe you're a colleague of the funder, this attitude isn't so hard to pull off, and you can make a memorable positive impression.

The more grant seeking you do, the more insightful your questions will become and the more trust and respect you will gain in the offices of funders. Eventually they will give you some useful details about why you were turned down. You may even get specific advice and an invitation to submit a revised proposal or a different proposal under their next deadline. In time as you develop relationships, some foundation staff might even agree to work with you on drafts of your major proposals before they go before the foundation's trustees.

The information you get about a rejection may not be the result you were originally hoping for, but it can help you move into the last phase of the five-step grant-seeking cycle, in which you will evaluate your experience.

IF YOU GOT THE GRANT

Congratulations! You should be proud. But while victory is sweet, the celebration is brief because you still have work to do to follow through on this grant. A funder has put trust in you, and you want the funder to know you appreciate it and will live up to your responsibilities and common goals. Although much of efficient grant seeking involves managing your time proactively instead of reactively, this is one circumstance where we advise you to drop everything to do a certain job. You should do the following:

→ Write a thank-you letter immediately.

→ If a foundation representative was particularly helpful to you during the grant process, call to express your thanks personally.

Next record tracking information:

→ Mark the result down on your Overall Tracking Form.

YOUR FOLLOW-UP PLAN

Communicating a prompt thank-you is important, but you can't stop there. An event we experienced illustrates the real value of continuing to follow through once you've gotten a grant. A funder gave our organization a one-year grant for our women's shelter and made it clear we would not be eligible to apply again the following year. We used the grant, and at the end of the year we followed up with a two-page letter on what a difference the funded program made in the lives of families surviving domestic violence. Not long afterward a foundation representative showed up unexpectedly at the shelter with a $25,000 check for another year. She said that our two-page letter was the greatest amount of information she had ever received from a grantee on how the foundation's money had been put to use.

Although it was surprising to learn how incommunicative our fellow nonprofits were, it was also great to learn how easy it can be to stand out. Simple courtesies like remembering a foundation's role in your success can encourage them to get involved with you all over again.

When you get a grant, you've at least temporarily persuaded a funder that your organization's interests are compatible with the funder's own and that you're capable of fulfilling your part of an equal deal. You want to satisfy that impression and build on it. Therefore it is vitally important to make follow-up communications with the funder, such as updates, year-end reports, and so on, *whether or not they are required by the funder.* In the short term they help you and the funder evaluate your program, let the funder know you appreciate the money, and, most important, let the funder know that the money is making a difference in a tangible way. In the long term follow-up materials communicate that your organization is responsible, produces results, and is worthy of continued, larger investments.

To get your follow-up on a specific grant started, you can use a form like Exhibit 12.1, the Grant Follow-Up Form, also available as a blank form in Exhibit A.8.

This form will allow you to track reporting and other activities related to this specific grant. So while you're enjoying gazing at the check you've received:

→ Fill out the top two sections of a Grant Follow-Up Form.

→ Conduct a fifteen-minute meeting with the funded program's director and possibly your CEO. In this meeting map out a specific plan of follow-up communications with a deadline for each.

Consider three kinds of follow-up in your plan: (1) any follow-up that is *required* by the funder, such as a signed agreement or year-end report; (2) any evaluation or follow-up materials you *promised* in your grant proposal (for example, products you promised in the evaluation section); (3) any *additional* points of communication you may think of, such as times and ways you can let the funder know the grant is making a difference.

A good way to plan is around program milestones. For example, if the grant supported a drama project, you might schedule a follow-up activity around opening night, planning to mail a playbill with the funder's name highlighted. You also want to consider your board in planning follow-up activities. If a board member was involved in supporting your proposal, that same board member should send a personal thank-you note or letter to his or her contact.

The scale and content of your follow-up should be appropriate to the grant. Too little may seem as though you've taken the money and run. Too much and you could appear to be fawning over the funder and spending undue time and energy on fundraising. If the grant was an emergency $1,000 so your homeless shelter could replace a broken refrigerator, you don't need to send much more than an initial thank-you letter and, a month or two later, a card with a photo of the new fridge in action, possibly being loaded by a volunteer. If the grant was $100,000 for an innovative homeless sheltering program, short quarterly status reports would not be out of order, including statistics about numbers of people helped and a few individual success stories. In almost all cases your follow-up plan should include a final report, regardless of whether the funder requires it.

When you've agreed on your follow-up plan, do this:

→ Document it by filling in the last section of the Grant Follow-Up Form, including a deadline or target date for each activity.

Exhibit 12.1. Grant Follow-Up Form

Use this form to plan your follow-up activities once a grant has been received.

Funder name ___The Chet & Olive Hofker Horticultural Fund___

Program funded ___Hosta test garden___

Person responsible for carrying out the funded program: ___Ginny, Master gardener___

Phone: ___999.999.3443___   E-mail ___virginia@gardenfriends.bbb___

Grant facts

Approximate grant dates	*Determination received*	*Check(s) received*	*Check(s) received*
Begin May 1, 2000	Date April 5, 2000	Date April 30, 2000	Date October 30, 2000
End April 30, 2001	Amount $10,000	Amount $5,000	Amount $5,000

Restrictions on spending

For plants and equipment only; they have a restriction against funding salaries.

Follow-up action timeline

Under "required by," circle who is requiring this action—the funder or your organization—and write in the date it is due.

Required by		*Action*	*Completed*	
Funder/Us	5.1.00	Thank-you letter & grant agreement	☑ 5/1/00	(date)
Funder/Us	11.00	Send thanks for 2nd check & photo of garden construction	☑ 11/20/00	(date)
Funder/Us	4.15.01	Hosta test garden opening reception; send invite & call	☑ 3/30/01	(date)
Funder/Us			❑	(date)
Funder/Us			❑	(date)
Funder/Us			❑	(date)
Funder/Us			❑	(date)

Final report due ___5.15.01___ form is theirs /(ours)

Final report mailed ☑ ___6.1.01___ (date)

→ Copy each of the follow-up deadlines from the Grant Follow-Up Form on to a new deadline card. File the deadline cards chronologically with your others.

→ Place the Grant Follow-Up Form in the appropriate "Funder" file.

Note that the deadline cards you've created for your follow-up activities go in the "Deadline" file, intermixed with cards for proposal deadlines. You need to treat these follow-up deadlines as seriously as proposal deadlines. When the time comes to meet them, consider sending any major follow-up communications through an internal review and editing process just the way you did with your grant proposal.

How to Drive the Follow-Up Process

Once a grant is received, you may find that the busy people at your organization are excited about the money but less willing to set aside time to meet with you. After all, their goal of funding has been achieved, and more immediate program needs begin to take precedence over fundraising. But you know that funding is not a one-shot process. It's cyclical and repetitive, and from your point of view you can see all the grants in the future that may or may not be made, depending on how you handle this one. Your job is to help others see that bigger picture and to encourage investing now in potential future grants.

Everyone should understand their roles. You, the grant seeker, are a communicator and an organizer. It is the program staff who are truly accountable for using the grant and fulfilling your organization's part of the deal. You will depend on the program staff for the material you need for follow-up communications like statistics and stories. If they do not provide you with information, or worse, do not take the requirements of the grant seriously and do not complete the proposed activities, you as grant seeker are not going to make up excuses or fantasies to tell funders.

When things go right, you can help the program staff portray the real *value* of their work, which can positively affect future funding at your agency. Talk about this early and often so that everyone begins to understand the ways you all depend on each other.

Work to get people to create your follow-up plans *together* in a meeting as described earlier. The program staff need to be invested in the follow-up plan and committed to the process so they will play their parts when the time comes. Don't be a stranger to them. Set aside part of each week to simply *talk* to program staff about what is going on in their world. Then when you see a follow-up deadline approaching, you can remind them of their obligations and stand a good chance of getting a timely answer. If your organization's staff are very busy or respond better to a formal reminder, make your request on something like the Staff Reminder Form (available as Exhibit A.9) or a similar form you create to use via e-mail. This demonstrates your serious commitment to follow-up and the importance of their responses.

Honesty

Even with the best of intentions, nonprofit programs sometimes have problems and unexpected changes. As a grant seeker who maintains open communication with other staff, you may learn about those problems and changes early in their development. It might then become your job—and a good idea—to communicate with the funder about them.

For example, a funded program might have trouble meeting its goals or might veer from its originally proposed intent or format. A project to install equipment may be delayed by a vendor or by unexpected problems with the building site, or a program may get started several months late due to changes in staffing. On the positive side a program may change dramatically as a result of new ideas or opportunities.

If a funded program is a few months off schedule but still moving along toward its ultimate goals, you can simply adjust your follow-up dates to match the new milestones. If a program is significantly late or is being substantially changed from the proposed program that was granted money, you should discuss this with the program staff and CEO. *Together* you should determine at what point you will contact your funder to request an extension or change in your grant scope or expenses. If you have logical reasons for changing or rescheduling a project and you communicate these, funders will most often find your reasonableness and openness commendable.

For example, our organization once received a sizeable grant to put new ceilings, carpet, and lighting into a community center that had not been renovated for decades. Our entire proposal focused on the increase in self-esteem that would be gained for our children when we installed new, clean, bright carpeting and proper lighting. But when our contractors went to work on the ceiling, they discovered hazardous asbestos inside.

Our organization asked the funder if we could use their grant for asbestos abatement—not the same kind of project as the one we first proposed. The foundation immediately understood why our priorities had changed and supported our new needs. They respected our openness and concern for our kids' safety, and later they made several larger grants to us. In this case we were able to use a real setback to cultivate a stronger funding relationship. We didn't try to hide the problem, which was an imminently practical approach (a problem this big would be hard to hide) and one that spoke to our integrity.

As usual the key in this situation was keeping truthful, compelling information flowing out of our office to the funder, to keep them engaged in our work. You can do this, too, but be sure to do so together with your CEO and with any board members who have personal contacts at the relevant foundation and may have endorsed your proposal. Even if your organization has problems that are more serious or more embarrassing, we're confident this principle is the one most compatible with long-term success in grant seeking.

WHAT'S NEXT

Whether or not you received a grant, you have set important systems in place and have begun building working relationships. You've made a positive impression with follow-up communication regardless of a grant maker's funding decision. Now you are ready to complete the grant-seeking cycle by taking stock of what you've learned.

step five **Evaluate** Your Results, Methods, and Opportunities

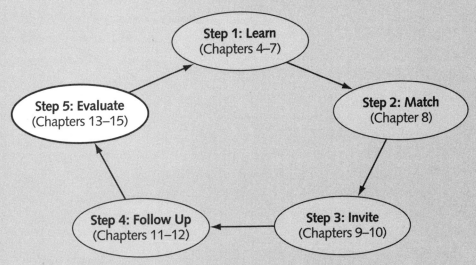

Step 1: Learn
(Chapters 4–7)

Step 2: Match
(Chapter 8)

Step 3: Invite
(Chapters 9–10)

Step 4: Follow Up
(Chapters 11–12)

Step 5: Evaluate
(Chapters 13–15)

Now that you have worked through a complete grant proposal, you evaluate how all the previous steps worked and how your methods can be improved. Why did you or didn't you get the grant? Was your work efficient enough to make getting the grant worthwhile? At this point you also strategize for the future. What are your next opportunities, and how should you pursue them? Armed with self-knowledge, you head into Step One again, ready to learn about any changes in your program, your community, and your next prospective funder's mission, before you invite them to invest in your organization.

Evaluate the Past, Strategize the Future

You've made it to the last step of the grant-seeking cycle. Just as they told you at high school graduation, this final event is also a new beginning. In Step Five you use your recent experience to adjust the strategies and techniques you'll use when you return to Step One and start work on another grant request.

There are several kinds of evaluating and strategizing you can do. Because you're running a steady, ongoing grant-seeking effort, the activity you'll always perform in Step Five is to decide which grant opportunity to pursue next. In this chapter you'll use the benefit of your experience to do that and begin the grant-seeking cycle all over again. We'll also suggest ways to evaluate your success and set goals for the future. In later chapters we'll cover topics that will become more important as you start working on multiple grant requests simultaneously. You'll learn to evaluate and streamline the way you work with others at your organization and manage your time more efficiently.

ASSESS YOUR OPPORTUNITIES AND RETURN TO STEP ONE

You've probably already started thinking about it: What funding opportunities should you go for next? You can use your "Deadline" file to prod your thinking on this subject and generally help you maintain control over the grant-seeking process.

The collection of cards in your "Deadline" file should have grown considerably by now. Ever since your first time through Step One of the grant-seeking cycle, you've been digging up leads, requesting funding guidelines, looking at funders' Web sites, and perhaps receiving grants for which you've scheduled follow-up activities. Rather quickly you will have accumulated dozens of cards, each representing a funder and a deadline; if you follow our system for long, you could accumulate hundreds.

Although you can't change most of the deadlines represented by those cards, you don't have to let deadlines sneak up on you and throw you into the crisis mode of the episodic grant seeker.

→ Take twenty minutes or so right now (and anticipate spending some time each week or so) to flip through the "Deadline" file and scan all the approaching opportunities.

→ During this session consider all your grant-worthy programs and projects, all your potential funders, and the upcoming deadlines in your file. Make educated decisions about which funding opportunities should be pursued now and which can be left on the back burner.

Let several factors play into your thinking. Timing is one. If you are a beginning grant seeker or are overhauling your grants effort, we suggest considering deadlines that are a few months off. If it's January, consider applying for deadlines in March or April. Although by now you are prepared to write a grant proposal in a day if necessary, you still want to guard yourself against delays caused by other people who are not yet used to your system or get called out of town at an inopportune time. Perhaps more important, starting early will allow you to proceed calmly, even if two or three major opportunities have deadlines on the same day.

Another factor is the strength of the matches between your projects and prospects. As you flip through your deadline cards, ask yourself things like, "From what I know so far, which funders seem the best bets for making a strong match? Are there any combinations of projects and funders that seem particularly natural, appropriate, or exciting?" As you know by now, you should apply only if you have a compelling match.

The feelings you have during this session will help determine the way you spend your time during your next trip through the grant-seeking cycle. If you have an exciting idea for a match between one of your organization's programs, your community's needs, and a funder's interests, make your interest official:

→ Tack the relevant deadline card up on the bulletin board in front of you, making it "active." Posting this card puts you and your coworkers on notice that you have something to deliver by that date.

In this case your next trip through the grant-seeking cycle will involve relatively little time in Step One. Because you already have a match in mind, it will be easy to concentrate your research on the specific program, funder, and community need involved. You will be able to spend a relatively high proportion of your time on Step Three, writing the proposal, meeting with foundation staff, and so on. But even if you feel like you know everything, do not skip Step One. Your information can usually be updated. For example, check in with your program director to see whether new stories or press clippings are available or whether community needs have changed.

If your brainstorming produces less-than-exciting results, your next trip through the grant-seeking cycle will necessarily involve more expansive research and substantial time in Step One and Step Two. Although you shouldn't need to learn much about your organization in general, you may want to write proposals for programs other than the one you've studied throughout this book. You'll also want to uncover more funding leads and investigate prospects before you can confidently post deadline cards on the wall.

EVALUATE YOUR EFFORTS AND SET GOALS

After a number of times around the grant-seeking cycle (perhaps six months or five or ten grant requests out and "verdicts" in), your Step Five will begin to include more than just evaluating opportunities and deciding what to apply for next. You will be able to look back and make an analysis of your work, considering questions such as, "Am I successful, in terms of the amount of money I raise, the percentage of grant requests I win, and so on?" The most appropriate way to evaluate your success may or may not involve such hard numbers.

If you were hired as a "grant writer," you might have been told more or less subtly that your first order of business was to raise enough money to pay your own salary. By now you should realize that a number picked out of the air, such as your salary, is an inappropriate standard with little relevance to your work. First of all, grants rarely pay for grant-seekers' salaries directly; as you know, they go to things like new or self-contained projects. Also the number and size of grants your organization receives is affected by factors beyond your control, meaning your own salary could be absurdly high or low as a goal.

It is unfortunate that too many grant seekers' goals are set for them in just such arbitrary ways and without their own input. This perpetuates damaging myths about grants and frustrates many a grant seeker, but it doesn't need to happen to you. By now you have the knowledge and skills to help set some meaningful goals for yourself. These are important because your goals are the number one way you'll know that your grant-seeking system is working. In this section we'll discuss various ways to evaluate how you're doing and set some realistic goals, both financial and nonfinancial, to give you something to strive for.

Success Rate

Inevitably someone will ask you what percentage of proposals you get funded, giving the impression that there is an ideal or standard rate. This impression is based on the myth that your powers as a writer are the sole reason grants are won or lost. You may want to take the opportunity to educate the person about grant seeking (which is sure to be appreciated).

You do control many factors relating to grant-seeking success, such as the number of proposals you send out, how well they are targeted, how meaningful and compelling they are, and how willing you are to call and visit foundation staff. The whole premise of this book is that developing productive habits in these areas can improve your success rate considerably—enough to make the work of grant seeking very worthwhile.

At the same time there are factors that as a grant seeker you can't control, such as how well your programs are designed, how well your organization followed up with funders before you worked there, and the volume and quality of competitive proposals received by foundations. We have had success rates of anywhere from 70 to 0 percent, and we were the same grant seekers every time. The variables were the programs and organizations for which we were working and the pool of other grant applicants.

Given the number of variables, your success rate statistic is not very informative by itself. But if you understand grant seeking, it isn't completely worthless either. It may provide some clues for your strategy. In general if you are receiving 50 percent of the grants you apply for, you are probably doing very well. If you receive any *more* than 50 percent, it may sound great, but it could be that you are being *too safe* with your efforts and missing out on new donors. (Remember that 100 percent of 1 is still just one grant.) You might want to send out more proposals, even if you are less comfortable with them. However, if you are receiving *much less* than 50 percent, you may not be targeting your proposals and presenting them in a clear, organized way; or your program may not be ready or appropriate for grants.

If you are near 0 percent success after a year of making a consistent effort like the one described in this book, it's time for some serious evaluation. It is unfortunate that some worthwhile programs just won't get grants. As a grant seeker you cannot work miracles. If your program is one of the kinds of projects foundations do not typically fund (such as a conference or ongoing program with no expansion or change) or is not sufficiently developed beyond the idea stage, you might not receive any grants no matter how good a grant seeker you are. Other situations that might keep you from winning grants, despite the best of efforts, are when your organization lacks credibility, when your program works against deeply held social mores or preconceptions, or when your programs address a need that (however unjustly) is not deemed worthy or important by most of the community. For example, we never received any grants for a well-designed disaster preparedness program and found later that a few foundations we approached believed that this issue should be handled by government, not by a private nonprofit.

If you are having far less success than you hoped for or expected, you'll have to take a hard look at your program to see if any of the situations just described apply to you. It may be that shifting your focus to corporate or individual donors makes sense or that another program or project within your organization would be better suited to grant seeking.

If your program is successful, prominent, and addresses a cause of great general concern or if it is new or expanding, it may be highly attractive for grants. If you work for a program like this, you may be able to set your goals much higher than you originally thought, and this will be clear from your results.

Financial Goals

Even though we see grant seeking as more than pursuing money, your immediate charge is to raise funds. Setting a realistic yet challenging annual financial goal is useful. Your goal shouldn't be so high that you feel hopeless and program staff walk the halls in the enchanted expectation they will have a large amount of funds to spend in the near future. At the same time you don't want to achieve your goal so easily that you have nothing left to work for.

To set financial goals for your grant seeking, remember that grants are given to programs, not to "grant writers." You can only get grants for the things your organization is *doing* that are *grant-worthy.* Therefore we suggest that a realistic but still inspiring goal will roughly correspond to the total cost of all the programs and project items you need that are truly grant-worthy. Because you are becoming adept at recognizing what is grant-worthy, and you have increasing knowledge about funders' practices and your organization's priorities, you must play an active role in calculating this figure.

→ Once per year sit down with your CEO, development director, and perhaps key program staff to set grant-seeking goals.

During this meeting review your organization's programs and define which ones are board and executive staff's priorities. Then review specific program plans and goals for the coming year, and note any major upcoming expansions, changes, new projects, or capital needs. You need to estimate how much money each of these expansions, changes, or purchases will cost and sum those costs into a single total.

The next step is key and is where your growing expertise comes in. *Subtract* from your total any projects that, based on all your knowledge, are not likely grant candidates. Examples might be your annual staff retreat at the coast or the budget for that half-baked program someone is still developing. Raising operating salaries $1 per hour may not make a great grant proposal (but could be covered by major giving or another area of the development effort), whereas purchasing a safe floor for your playground sounds like a compelling, cohesive, and very grant-worthy project.

The resulting number will be a reasonable starting point for your annual grant-seeking goal. You can adjust it further, based on your detailed knowledge, work load, priorities, and circumstances. Your final goal could be less than your own salary, but in most circumstances it will be a lot more.

Nonfinancial Goals

You should set nonfinancial goals to complement your financial ones. These can give you a sense of progress and satisfaction while you wait long months to see if your proposals have been funded or when you fail to win grants due to factors beyond your control.

To make nonfinancial goals meaningful, think about the activities that are the elements of effective grant seeking, such as learning about new leads and inviting foundations to fund your programs. Next convert those activities into measurable or verifiable accomplishments and assign end dates. Some goals of this kind include "making ten new foundation or corporate contacts this quarter," "meeting 100 percent of my follow-up reporting deadlines this year," "mailing out twenty proposals this year (whether or not they are funded)," or "doing that particularly difficult proposal to the XYZ foundation, due on May 1st." They should be things you can point to and tell your supervisor about with pride, whether or not you've gotten any checks in.

→ Come up with three measurable, nonfinancial goals for the next few months or year, and write them in here:

 _____

One-Year Review

Although they can be valuable for your organization, grants are rarely the fastest way to raise money. If your organization has programs you believe are grant-worthy, it could easily take six to twelve months of steady effort, even if it is just a few well-spent hours per week, before you have enough evidence to conduct a meaningful evaluation of how you're doing. During your first year you can use this book and the nonfinancial goals you develop yourself to provide a sense of progress. Then do this:

→ At the end of each year review your financial and nonfinancial goals.

→ During this review create an internal, end-of-year report for your coworkers or supervisors.

From documents like your Overall Tracking Form you should be able to total the number and dollar amount of grants you've applied for and those you've received. From your other notes you can estimate how close you've come to meeting nonfinancial goals, such as new contacts made. Comparing nonfinancial and financial results might be revealing. For example, if you've won 75 percent of the four grants you applied for while you met one hundred foundation staff people, you're probably concentrating too much on networking and not enough on sending out proposals.

If your annual review reveals unsatisfactory results, there are steps you can take. If your success rate seems too low, call a few foundation staff people. Ask them to sit down with you and help you understand how they see your proposals from their side of the table. Stress that you are not trying to get a grant at this time but are trying to learn and evaluate your work. Then stick by this promise and don't ask for money at this meeting. It could be a remarkable learning experience.

You may also want to conduct a more in-depth review of the guidelines and tax forms of several funders who have declined grants to your organization. Write down any key points you find in common. For example, if nine out of ten funders you applied to this year make the majority of their "education" grants to universities and yours is an early childhood learning program, you may have found your problem and can refocus your efforts and try again. The point is to be aware of your results, be they successes or disappointments, so you can adjust your efforts accordingly.

CELEBRATE SUCCESS

While you're learning from your victories, feel free to enjoy them. Grant funding might result from steady and rational work, but it's not guaranteed. When you, your program staff, and your volunteers work together to create the right proposal for the right funder, and a check comes in that will support an important new project, buy an industrial freezer, make a wish come true for a child with a life-threatening illness, or launch an exciting new computer lab, you should congratulate yourselves and recognize everyone who contributed.

As organizer of the grant-seeking effort, you'll be at the center of this activity. It is often your happy task to call program staff and tell them you've received funding. You may then need to thank the people who contributed to the proposal with their input or labor. This can be very simple. For example, consider listing all their names in a memo with the grant news and circulating it around your whole organization. A more personal touch might be called for with the assistant or volunteer who spent a week working with you on the proposal. Perhaps you could take that person out to lunch or give him or her movie tickets. Enjoying your successes and recognizing hard work will go a long way toward keeping your whole organization invested in the grant-seeking effort.

Personalize Your Grant-Seeking Cycle

If this book has been right for you, by now you have new confidence about grant seeking and a mean set of grant-seeking tools under the hood of your file cabinet. Your organization's grants program is under control, and you are poised to enjoy the benefits of a good system.

One benefit is freed-up time. Now that you've made the hard investment of setting up your system and doing initial research about your community and your organization, you should be able to get more grant proposals out in a month than the average grant seeker does in half a year. However, to realize that kind of productivity, you need to do two things: (1) plan to work efficiently in the coming months, and (2) decide to do meaningful things with the time you save. (We hope you'll pencil in a lot of sleep.)

In this chapter we lead you through a part of Step Five that you'll only need to do occasionally: revising your general schedule. Our intention isn't to drive you to set down a day-by-day, hour-by-hour schedule in your day planner. Rather we want you to have a good sense of how you will divide your time among all the varied and yet recurring tasks that make up effective grant seeking. Think of this as a scenic tour through your grant-seeking calendar.

YOUR OWN GRANT-SEEKING CYCLE

In this book we've frequently suggested that you set aside specific times each week or month for this or that activity. Now that you've had experience with all those activities, it should be possible for you to plan how to spend your grant-seeking time for the foreseeable future. We've gathered up all those tasks and arranged them in the rough order we think you should perform them—daily, weekly, monthly, yearly, and so on. To ensure that you're covering all the bases, you should write in the next two dates on which you plan to perform each task. This will give you a detailed guide for the next six to twelve months. After that you'll be an expert and won't need help from books like this.

Our suggested frequencies are based on the assumption that you work twenty to forty hours per week on grant seeking. If you're working less than that, you should still go through with the exercise, adjusting the frequencies somewhat. For example, daily items might be weekly ones if you only work on grant seeking one day per week. Regardless of how much time you have to put into grant seeking, you already know that the key to success is consistency.

YOUR CYCLE WHEN THINGS GET COMPLICATED

While we were walking you through the grant-seeking cycle for the first time, we asked you to focus on just one program and funding prospect. Now that your training wheels are off, you will likely be faced with multiple deadlines, several funding priorities competing for your attention, and several written proposals going through various stages of the editing process at once. In the real world of grant seeking, proposals do not line up and wait their turn; things get messy. This is why you should learn each step of the grant-seeking cycle solidly before you start overlapping cycles, that is, learning about one project while writing a proposal for another and doing research for a third, all in one week.

Once you are ready to tackle multiple projects and deadlines, you should practice a very important habit we've mentioned before: dividing your time into blocks of work. You should always do similar tasks together to save the mental time it takes to switch gears and to ensure you do everything that needs to be done. Keep using your folders as holding places for work until it is the right time. Try to set aside time each day, week, month, and year for the activities that make up your system. We'll help you get started:

Daily (or Most Frequent) Activities

These are the things that take up the bulk of your time and effort. Write your next two dates for each job on the lines provided. However, make sure to leave some time for less frequent but equally important work that we'll cover next.

→ Research and write proposals. This includes thinking about funder-program matches, making calls, attending meetings, writing narratives, creating budgets, moving drafts through the editing process, and mailing proposals.

✍ _____

→ Follow up on grants received and rejected. This includes creating follow-up communications for grants you have received and updating your Overall Tracking Form.

✍ _____

→ Learn about your community and the world of grant making. This includes reading newspapers and grant-related periodicals.

✍ _____

→ As you go along, put away everything that already has its own place, such as "Funder" files.

✍ _____

Weekly (or Fairly Frequent) Activities

Many of these activities touch on future grant opportunities; these will keep your grant seeking moving ahead. Most consume little time, especially considering their potential. Write your next two dates for each in the space provided.

→ Scan deadline cards, looking ahead several months.

✍ _____

→ Look up new funding leads, and put them in your "Funders to Contact" file.

✍ _____

→ Call or e-mail your new leads to get their guidelines and information.

✍ _____

➔ Download information from leads that have Web sites.

☞ _____

➔ Review materials that have arrived in the mail or you have downloaded.

☞ _____

➔ Create new file folders for your unsorted material.

☞ _____

➔ Check in with at least one of your organization's program directors or key volunteers.

☞ _____

➔ Notify your boss and coworkers about grant proposals mailed out and any grants received.

☞ _____

➔ Upon receipt of each grant thank the funder, and create your follow-up plan and follow-up deadline cards.

☞ _____

Monthly or Quarterly Activities

Many of these activities are the kind of periodic maintenance you will need to perform on your grant-seeking system to keep it relevant to current conditions and efficient in operation. Write your next two dates for each in the spaces provided.

➔ Conduct research on community conditions and the latest statistics.

☞ _____

➔ Replenish copies of all base materials.

☞ _____

➔ Update financial statements in your "Organization and Program" files.

☞ _____

→ Copy your Overall Tracking Form to others so that they will be on the lookout for related calls and mail.

☞ _____

→ Provide your board with a list of grants pending and grants received.

☞ _____

→ Provide the board with a list of trustees of foundations that are currently on your radar screen.

☞ _____

→ Call or meet with at least one foundation staff person.

☞ _____

Semiannual Activities

These activities are meant to keep you working in sync with your organization's management and leadership. Write your next two dates for each in the spaces provided.

→ Remind your organization's management team of how your system works and how your office is set up.

☞ _____

→ Remind your management team to give you updated grant-seeking priorities.

☞ _____

Annual Activities

These activities stress evaluating your past work and getting ready for the next year.

→ Update your organizational resume, program resume, and other base materials, such as annual audits.

☞ _____

→ Create an annual report for your grant-seeking work.

☞ _____

→ Set your financial and nonfinancial goals for the coming year.

✍ _____

We think that balancing your grant seeking time between all these kinds of activities will help you be more productive. But for better or worse, you are not the only person who influences your work schedule. In the next chapter you set some ground rules for making your interactions with coworkers easier and more fruitful.

Set Your Grant-Seeking Ground Rules

As your experience in grant seeking grows, you'll learn that the dynamics of your interactions with coworkers can have a big impact on the number and quality of grant proposals you send out. For example, you rely on your organization's program directors for information and reviews of your proposals; they rely on you to coordinate communications and visits with funders; meanwhile you all have other responsibilities that take up your time. Everyone involved will benefit from understanding what is expected of them and knowing how they'll be kept in the loop, especially as you start moving through the grant cycle more quickly and have multiple proposals in different stages of the cycle simultaneously.

An important part of Step Five (but one you'll have to do only once or twice per year) is sitting down with your coworkers to set ground rules that define the way you'll work together. In this chapter we'll lead you through this discussion in detail. The main points you need to resolve are also available on a blank form (Exhibit A.10 in Resource A). Feel free to copy this form, bring it with you to the meeting, and use it to record your new policies.

You'll probably want to think of the results as a kind of rough draft to be tested and changed later. If you've only been through the grant-seeking cycle a few times, you're probably not ready to set anything in stone, especially when it comes to key decisions like who sets fundraising priorities and how development and program staff interact. But it is a good time to start thinking about these issues. When you ramp your grant-seeking work up to a more intense pitch, you don't want misunderstandings to hold you back.

THE INITIAL SUMMIT

You'll need to hold two meetings to set your ground rules. The first is a summit with the one or two people in your office who have the authority to set fundraising priorities and direct other staff to work with you. Depending on the size and complexity of your organization, this is likely to include the CEO, the development director, or both. If you work in a large organization, limit this meeting to the very few managers who are directly involved in your grants effort. If you work in a one-person shop, sit down with a cup of coffee and hold this "meeting" with yourself.

→ Schedule this summit meeting. You might need about forty-five minutes of everyone's time. Write in the scheduled date and time here:

 _____

During this meeting your goal is to create a basis of understanding on a few overarching issues that will affect all your work. There's no need to resolve these issues for all time, but your solutions should apply to at least the next few months. It's also a good time for you to ask any nagging questions about your own job responsibilities, so you might want to take your job description, if you have one, along.

Set Priorities

You won't have much trouble figuring out your fundraising priorities if your organization has only one program. But most organizations have more than one program or project they want to fund with grants. Unless you have unlimited time and unlimited funding prospects, you will need to pick and prioritize among them. To do that you need direction from above. Your job is to raise money based on your organization's actual needs and aspirations, not to discern or invent reasons to raise money. And for reasons described at length in Chapter One, it should not be your job to design new projects and programs for the purpose of raising money. So ask the people assembled:

✔ Who sets priorities and decides which programs I will raise funds for?

✔ What are the top five programs or projects for which I should seek grants? If you had to pick, which would be the very first priority?

✔ How often will we meet to revisit these priorities?

The exercise of ranking your programs and projects in order of grant-seeking priority may be difficult for your group, but it reflects some important realities of the grant-seeking process. Just asking your organization's leaders to do it reinforces the idea that you as the grant seeker cannot and should not be responsible for determining organizational priorities by yourself. In most small organizations the CEO sets priorities after planning and strategizing with the board of directors and program staff.

The challenge of determining your first-priority program may cause your leaders to protest that "all our programs are important" or "they all have equally important elements." However, as a successful grant seeker you target your approaches. Most funders have policies against submitting multiple proposals in one year, so you need to make the most of each annual opportunity. A great majority of funders discourage multiple-choice proposals in which you show them your range of needs and ask them to pick. Grant makers expect you to bring your top-priority need to them. In your summit meeting you prepare for these realities of grant seeking.

Asking questions about *updating* priorities reinforces the reality that priorities can and will change as your organization grows, learns, meets goals, and moves on to new ones. Because grants can take up to a year to propose and receive, as grant seeker you will need to be aware of any changes in program priorities, such as special expansions or capital projects, long before they are slated to occur.

If you are seeking funding for just one program, you may not need to update your priorities more than once per year. You might do it less often than that. We worked with one client—an organization that implements one large program—whose staff and board organized their fundraising in "campaigns" of three years each. Each campaign had a single goal; the first was to reach ten thousand clients; the next was to expand statewide. Inside the three-year campaign periods, we always knew what we were raising funds for and what was most important. For another client—an organization running ten different programs at once—we needed updates on program priorities every six months, which is the bare minimum amount of time we recommend allotting to a grant-seeking priority to get results.

Define Responsibilities and Roles

Your summit meeting may include people you have already worked with on grant seeking, such as the CEO, a program director, or board member. Now is the time to start formally dividing responsibilities and creating expectations for how different people work together. Formalizing your roles will help everyone feel secure about how grant seeking will work. For example, you will be assured that you're not expected to be a magician, pulling new program plans out of a hat. And program staff will be assured that their expertise is valued and they will not be overlooked in the process. Ask your CEO questions like these:

✔ Who designs new programs and projects that might be funded by grants?

✔ How will the development staff work together to support grant seeking and other forms of fundraising?

✔ How will you (the CEO) be involved in grant-seeking work?

✔ How will board members be involved in grant-seeking work?

As we've stressed, new programs and projects are most effectively and appropriately designed by program staff. However, as grant seeker there are several ways you can help. For example, you may act as a facilitator, helping program staff ask themselves questions about program goals (as you did in Chapter Four).

The way grant-related duties are split up among the CEO, the grant seeker, and the rest of the development staff varies among organizations. In the smallest organizations, the CEO, the development staff, and the grant seeker may be the same person. In larger organizations the CEO often provides strategy and close supervision of the grant-seeking process, or that job may be done by the development director. Your job description and hiring interviews may have already indicated who provides direct supervision of your work. If you're not sure, now is the time to clarify what parts of the grant-seeking process the CEO and development director want to be involved in.

The board's role also varies in relation to your organization's size. In most established organizations, the board of directors' job is to monitor the big picture, that is, where the organization is headed; there is no need for the board to review individual proposals. In newer or very small organizations the board may be active enough in fundraising to write some of the material you will use. Discuss with the CEO how board members might be involved in your work. In just about every case you will want board members to stay informed about grants and be available to advocate for specific proposals when you ask them.

THE SECOND SUMMIT

Your initial summit meeting should have provided you with some valuable direction for your next few months of grant seeking, but you still need to flesh out some specific expectations for the way grant-seeking work will flow. Arrange a second summit meeting, this time including program managers or others who are most likely to be called upon to contribute to or review your work during the grant-seeking cycle. This would include your organization's leaders from the last meeting, as well as the leaders of the programs or projects that have high priority for your grant-seeking work.

→ Schedule this second meeting. You will probably need between one and two hours. Write in the scheduled date and time here:

 _____

When this meeting time comes, your goal is to orient everyone to the five steps of the grant cycle and establish clear divisions of labor and expectations for collaboration at each step. We'll walk you through the major topics in the sections that follow.

Discuss Step One: Learn

As you learned in Chapters Four through Seven, successful grant seeking depends on your knowledge of your organization and its needs, your community, and potential funders. Therefore the bulk of your grant-seeking work happens long before you ever write a proposal. Most people don't know this about the grant-seeking cycle, so you will want to clarify this for your coworkers and discuss the following issues:

✔ Who plans programs and conducts research about specific program needs, such as the cost of equipment or the number of people we want to serve?

✔ Who conducts research about community needs?

✔ Who conducts research about funders?

By now you know how we feel about program planning. We think it should be carried out by program staff who can then relay their plans and share their expertise with you, the grant seeker. Your coworkers may have different expectations, having had experiences with grant seekers who invented programs for them or having absorbed the myth that grant writers can get them money for nothing. Now that you have a bit of experience to draw on, clarify your role in program planning. You may want to describe yourself as a facilitator whose job is to bring programs before funders and invite them to invest.

While the topic of program planning is on the table, talk specifically about budgets. In many organizations, especially very small, busy ones, the grant seeker is expected to create budgets, and you will want to create tailored versions of budgets for your proposals. However, we recommend that the raw numbers behind these tailored budgets should come from program staff. Pricing the equipment, staff costs, and other expenses of programs is part of program planning, and program staff are the experts in what it actually costs to do their work. It's in their interest for these numbers to be accurate, because they will have to live with the established budget should a grant come through. We recommend a formal policy that places the responsibility for program budgeting on the people who plan the programs. If your organization would rather you handle this job, formalize it up front so you know to include time for it in your future travels through the grant cycle.

We think research should largely be the grant seeker's responsibility. Taking charge of funder research in Step One will be critical to your success. You are the one who needs to have in-depth knowledge of your funders in order to find compelling unions of funder missions and your programs.

You will want to be involved in research into community conditions and needs as well. However, program staff are in a position to have state-of-the-art information about their areas of expertise. They may even generate their own original research in the field or make presentations for which they compile useful data. You may want to agree that program staff will keep you informed of any reports, news stories, or new developments in their fields.

Discuss Step Two: Match

Your coworkers may not be aware of some of the realities of the grant-seeking process, for example, that not all needs are grant-worthy or that decisions are made on several levels before you seriously pursue a grant proposal. For example, your CEO might set funding priorities, whereas you make decisions about specific proposals within those priorities. It is important that everyone understands the general logic behind grant-seeking decisions and knows who makes decisions on each level. That way if they have ideas or problems (for example, if they feel their program is not receiving enough attention), they can approach the appropriate party to discuss them.

→ Clarify how your organization settles on which grant proposals to pursue, including who sets fundraising priorities and what kinds of needs are grant-worthy, as well as the process of matching.

→ Set a clear policy about who can float grant ideas with funders and make other informal requests.

We recommend that once fundraising priorities are set, you be put in charge of matching and communicating with prospects (albeit with the collaboration or supervision of your CEO or development director). As grant seeker you will have knowledge about funders that other staff people don't have, and you will have dispensed with myths about grant seeking that your coworkers may still believe. Too often we've seen program staff pitch ideas to funders who are visiting for a tour and ask for something utterly inappropriate, given the funder's mission; or worse, they may ask for way too little money and then get it. Once we allowed a coworker to dictate the amounts we requested from several key funders, even though we thought they were too high; we were declined for every one. But we learned a valuable lesson: the time we spent *learning* made us best qualified to do the *matching*.

Discuss Step Three: Invite

This part of the grant-seeking cycle has the most details that need to be worked out with your coworkers, because this is where the written proposal is prepared and reviewed. Grants almost always require a written request, so you need to be clear about the nuts and bolts of how a match gets turned into a proposal, as well as other invitations to the funder. So discuss these topics:

✔ Who needs to approve making a formal request of a funder? Does this change with the size of the grant proposed?

✔ Who will be involved in the proposal writing and editing process and exactly how?

✔ How do each of you prefer to receive draft grant text (e-mail? hard copy?), and how long (realistically) do you need to review proposal text?

✔ Who is approved to sign grant applications?

✔ Who will make initial phone calls or other communications with funders and generally be their point of contact?

Depending on how your organization works, you may want to have two kinds of approvals required: (1) approval of a grant concept before it is turned into a proposal and (2) approval of specific grant proposals before they are mailed. In the first case you may want to set a policy that varies with the amount of the grant in question. As grant seeker you should be able to initiate proposals for under a certain dollar amount, say $10,000, without any permission, simply on the basis of your experience and investment in learning. If your organization is very formal in its procedures, you may want to set other levels that require specific approvals, for example, from program directors at $25,000 and from the CEO for any proposal over $50,000 (or any levels appropriate to your budget and experience with grants). This will keep any inappropriate grant concepts from getting past the idea stage, and it can be a tool for you in the future, if and when enthusiastic people in your organization want to send out proposals you feel are ill-advised.

Once you proceed past the idea stage, each proposal should be approved through an editing process like the one we went through in Chapter Ten. Think back to that process and what worked and didn't work. Your goal is to create an editing process that makes sense for your organization and you can live with for the next several months.

Set ground rules about who will write grant proposal text. Usually that's what you're hired for, but you may rely on program staff to write any technical portions of text, say, for a computer hardware request. Discuss exactly who must participate in reviewing and approving proposal text before it is sent out. At a minimum this will include one person other than you, usually the CEO, but we try to never include more than three people. Set a standard amount of time each of these people will be given to respond to draft proposals, say two weeks or two days, so your system won't get bogged down in the editing process. Also talk about how many chances each person will get to review and edit a proposal before it is mailed (we recommend just once, for the sake of speed and efficiency). Finally, discuss your ability as grant seeker to "skip" any reviewer who is not available for an extended period or at a critical time. For example, you may set a simple policy that you can only skip people in the editing loop with the CEO's permission.

Some foundations' application forms specify whose signature is required, for example, the CEO's or board president's. If not so specified, the CEO is almost always the first choice to sign correspondence with funders, grant proposals, cover letters, and forms. You might make exceptions when someone on the staff has had a meeting or conversation with a funder or knows a foundation representative well. Because signatures are essential for grant proposals, you'll want to create a backup plan in case your signer is unavailable when a deadline is nearing. For example, if the CEO is absent, the board president can sign in his or her absence.

The grant seeker is most often the primary point of contact for foundations, although you may sometimes call on the CEO or a board member to make an initial telephone call to a particularly important funding lead, or you may ask someone else to take over as point of contact with a particular funder later in the process. For example, this may happen if a program director makes a strong connection with a foundation trustee during a tour, and you decide to formally hand the contact responsibility over to that director. At this stage it may be simplest to set a ground rule that you're the first contact with any foundation unless you formally decide otherwise on a case-by-case basis.

Discuss Step Four: Follow Up

As you learned in Chapter Eleven, it's important to keep key people informed of the requests you have out to potential funders. One common scenario is a funder calling an organization to ask a specific question regarding a proposal. Your CEO and program staff shouldn't be caught defenseless. If you end up getting a grant, there are also matters of courtesy and accountability to plan for. So ask your coworkers:

✔ Who needs access to and understanding of foundation files?

✔ Who needs hard copies or electronic copies of proposals after they have been mailed?

✔ Who keeps the board and other staff up-to-date regarding proposals in progress?

✔ Who is responsible for our growing relationships with funders? Who sends thank-you's and receipts and produces follow-up communications?

The grant-seeking system you are setting up is an asset for your whole organization to use, and certain files can be accessible to program staff and other interested parties. For example, the community information you gather may be more than some program staff themselves gather and may inform their planning. You may be the only person at your organization who has taken time to learn about other nonprofits in your field. Because you seek grants up to a year before a planned project goes into effect, you may be gathering project details in time for them to be useful to your development colleagues who work with corporate or individual donors. As we've discussed before, we recommend that you keep your filing system simple enough for almost anyone to understand.

Although you may want to openly share your "Community" and "Organization and Program" files, "Funder" files are often the official record your organization keeps on what are essentially contracts with foundations. They often contain sensitive information about people's giving decisions, yet they need to be available to any staff person who may have to field a funder's questions. Decide who needs access to "Funder" files (usually program directors, other development staff, and the CEO). Make it your job to communicate with these people about your file system, once you have it set up. At a few organizations where we've worked, we've given a short tour of our filing systems every three months or so as part of regular management meetings. (If you are concerned about people returning files or respecting your system, you may want to set a ground rule that you will assist them in finding things unless it is an emergency and you're out of the office. Only you can make this determination.)

As a grant seeker you'll be proud of your finished proposals and excited about the potential income; you'll want to make sure everyone in the organization is knowledgeable. However, you don't want to invite dozens of people to critique your work on an ongoing basis. Limit your handouts of proposal copies to those who need them. In our experience this includes the program director and the CEO or development director.

In our experience people don't tend to keep all the papers or electronic files you send to them, even if they've requested them. In the end you may find that no one needs personal copies. Often at small organizations the paper file copy and the electronic copy the grant seeker saves are the only proposal copies that need to be retained by anyone. As long as people know how to access your files, they may not need to double up on their own.

We often provide brief monthly lists of proposals and their status to other development staff people, program staff members, and board members. These communications are critical to a healthy grants system because they keep ideas and information flowing among parties who might be able to make use of them and complement your work. At your second summit meeting, make sure you talk about any communications expected of you and discuss whether there is anyone to assist you. For example, sometimes there is a staff person who regularly sends out board packets and could include your brief report. In Chapter Eleven we discussed specific reports we recommend. Choose a couple of basic reports to schedule into your grant-seeking system for the next several months. You can always adjust as you learn more about your own style and your coworkers' expectations.

Even if communications with a funder are signed by the CEO or board president, they are often initiated and prepared by the grant seeker. You will likely be responsible for driving all communications to foundation funders, including official thank-you letters for each grant and other follow-up letters, cards, invitations, and any required reports (unless you work in a large organization with a department or person who handles all thank-you's and with whom you should coordinate closely).

Discuss when others will be called on to work with you. For example, you will often have to approach program staff for information about their progress toward their goals or their actual expenditures. Those who handle organizational finances may be called upon to provide accounting or receipts for a final report to a foundation. You'll want to notify these people well ahead of time that this will likely happen, so it's not a surprise when the time comes.

Discuss Step Five: Evaluate

As we discussed in Chapter Thirteen, it is important to look forward for new funding opportunities on a regular basis, and it is equally important and informative to look back and assess your recent efforts. Discuss new funding ideas and evaluation of past work with your coworkers:

✔ What should people do with grant ideas? How can they find out what I'm working on?

✔ Who sets grant goals for the year? How often will they be updated?

✔ Are any reports expected of me in addition to the proposal lists I distribute? If so, how often should I distribute them, and what should they include?

People you work with who care about your programs, from full-time staff to once-a-month volunteers, will have ideas about grants. They may read about them in the newspaper or hear about them from friends (who could turn out to be valuable contacts for you to initiate new business relationships). It's hard to tell at first which ideas will bear fruit. When the Bill and Melinda Gates Foundation made a $1-million grant to a Portland homeless youth shelter, every one of the clients we worked for asked us to write a letter of inquiry to the Gateses, none of which resulted in funding. However, when a Salvation Army staff person came to us with news of a grant opportunity at Microsoft that she had heard about through her sales representative, we worked together on a proposal that resulted in over $1 million worth of donated software.

Ask people to give you their ideas in writing or by e-mail. If you ask for ideas in writing, let people know they can simply be handwritten notes, nothing formal. The notes should include the funder's name and why that funder came to mind. Have a place people can put their notes (not on your chair). Then when you receive ideas, put them into your "Funders to Contact" file to ensure that they enter your system and get considered.

At your second summit meeting or during tours of your office, explain about your deadline cards and let your coworkers know they can always come in and see what you are working on by checking the bulletin board. This will encourage them to stay involved in grant seeking in an appropriate way by contributing their ideas, getting materials to you in a timely manner, and being supportive of you when you have a lot of deadlines on the wall.

Usually someone you report to (the CEO, development director, or even the board, depending on the size of your organization) will have a dollar goal in mind that they want you to reach. We talked about this in Chapter Thirteen, and by now you probably are aware of your financial grant goals and a few nonfinancial goals as well. If you haven't been formally notified of your goals during your hiring process or as part of your planning for taking on grant seeking, set a separate time to work through Chapter Thirteen together with your supervisor. At your second summit meeting, simply clarify who has the authority and responsibility to set your goals as of now and how often the goals will be reviewed and updated. This can be covered quickly, and it's positive for your coworkers to hear. It helps them realize you are not working in a vacuum and "playing God" with their programming dollars, and helps them understand how large your overall goals and responsibilities are.

In addition to the lists of pending grant requests you pledged to copy to board members and coworkers, talk about any results-oriented reports expected of you. These may include quarterly grant totals and an annual report. Try to agree on a reasonable limit to the reports being asked for, so they don't become the focus of your work and take precedence over seeking funding. For example, a monthly total is easy to provide, whereas a weekly journal of all your tasks would be excessive and take your focus off fundraising.

We were once working at a grant-seeking job for eight months before the development director expressed her wish that we'd give her a monthly rather than a quarterly report with grant dollar totals. She had to complete a monthly report for the CEO, and the quarterly totals we'd been providing her were not what she needed. We could have done a much better job for her and made her reports easier to complete and more accurate if we'd talked about her needs sooner. Covering this at your second summit meeting will help you do a better job.

Finally, wrap up the meeting by asking:

✔ When will we meet next to revisit these issues?

At the end of a long and detailed meeting, talk of the next meeting often gets dropped out of exhaustion and time constraints. But this is an important question, and we hope you can discuss it before the summit breaks up for lunch and people move on to other work. We recommend you give yourselves six months or longer to work with the ground rules you've just set up but that you do agree on a month when you will meet again. Then stick by your plan. If you say something like, "We'll just see how it goes," you may never get around to reviewing your work interactions, and small, nagging problems could become big ones that seriously affect your grants progress.

HOW TO WRITE UP YOUR GROUND RULES

Your two summit meetings have probably given you and your coworkers a great deal to think about. Although nothing is set in stone, do try to achieve basic, initial agreement on these issues. You can work with this agreement and test it during the period before your next meeting. Once you've achieved this basic agreement, make a formal expression of your grant-seeking policies and procedures:

➔ Use your notes from your two summit meetings to fill in Exhibit A.10, Grant-Seeking Ground Rules

➔ After you get approval from your CEO, give copies of the ground rules to all who need them.

This document can't guarantee that your collaboration with your coworkers will always be exactly what you desire. We're confident, though, that it will help you and your coworkers know what to expect from one another. It will also help you limit the number of people involved in the grants process, keeping proposals from getting bogged down by committee review. The investment you've made in these summit meetings will pay off when key people cooperate with your grant-seeking effort and you are able to stay on your toes and meet your goals.

Get Inspired
All Over Again

Grow from Efficiency to Expertise

Grant seeking is an occupation in which you will be constrained by time, inundated with information, and perhaps besieged by fears and misconceptions. Yet as a grant seeker you have the potential to learn about wonderful programs, raise money for the community, and make dreams come true. Through this book we hope we have inspired you by demonstrating a perspective and a method you can use to get past the challenges of the grant-seeking world and reach your full potential.

The perspective you should know by now. It's the idealistic but productive notion that grants can be fair deals between colleagues rather than the fruit of noble grace or intrigue. The method is based on a set of work habits that are compatible with the basic nature of grant seeking and the practices of funders. Those habits will already be familiar to you because throughout the book we've been harping on ideas like *targeting* your proposals and *limiting* the number of people involved in the grant-seeking process. These are the practices that keep you from wasting time on inappropriate tasks and leave you free to build the kind of relationships that can result in more grants—in short, the habits that make you effective.

In this chapter we'll discuss all those habits in one place and show how you can use the same concepts to grow from an efficient grant seeker into an expert.

HABIT: CYCLE

You already know that foundations make grants in repetitive calendar cycles. Your work has a repetitive quality, too, because the same kinds of tasks—conducting research, writing, interviewing program staff, making telephone inquiries, and so on—need to be performed again and again for each grant request, with slight variations. You take advantage of this repetition in your work. Rather than doing things as they fall on your desk (or get placed on your chair), you cycle through your work, dividing your time into blocks so you can do each task without distraction.

Over a longer term you will begin to see cycles in your relationships with individual funders. After you've won a grant, some foundations will not be interested in funding you again for a few years. However, many others will be happy to consider your applications at least once a year, sometimes more frequently, as long as each proposal is for a different project. We've even heard from foundation trustees who asked, "Why hasn't your organization come to us again for another grant? We were expecting to hear from you this year." If you have something grant-worthy, there's no reason to disappoint such a colleague.

If you're not sure whether a new grant request is appropriate, analyze your relationship with the funder. Based on your conversations with the funder's staff, do you think you're sending too few or too many proposals? You may want to call your contacts there and ask how often they are willing to consider your proposals for different projects or even the same project over time. Your proposals to each funder should form a logical sequence, one building on another and varying in amounts, not necessarily always growing.

Seeking grants from the same funders on a recurring basis will be easiest if your organization has a variety of programs or often expands or creates models of successful projects and therefore has a lot of grant-worthy needs. Most often your consistent funders will be local and regional foundations who get to know you well and are committed to making grants in your geographic area.

We call this kind of funding your annual fund of grants, and building one is similar to building an annual fund from individual donors. You need to consistently add new prospects to your list and maintain your contact with existing donors so they continue and upgrade their giving. But even with this larger perspective one thing hasn't changed. You still need a good reason for sending each proposal to each funder. You still need a match, and by taking a systematic and logical approach you will find one time and again.

HABIT: ANTICIPATE

Because grant making and grant seeking are cyclical, a lot about what you do is predictable. By anticipating the kind of work and issues you will be confronted with, you save yourself a lot of trouble and get more done. In proposal writing you anticipate the information you will be asked for over and over and create base materials to express it, so you don't waste time and brain power writing the same thing ten or twenty times. On a mental level you anticipate the stress of a fundraising job. You manage deadlines with devices like posted deadline cards and the expectations that others have of you with things like your grant-seeking ground rules.

As you become more experienced, you might come to anticipate that your job is so unique few other people understand it. You may find that you especially value the help of two kinds of people: other grants experts and friends and family. It's important to know someone else who does what you do. You can seek out other grants people through the Internet and professional organizations. You can share successful ideas and approach problems together. After a while you find that people are seeking you out to be their adviser and mentor in grant seeking. You're not shy about these opportunities; they can always help you learn more. Family and friends can help you by giving a fresh outsider's response to a draft proposal or serving as a sounding board. But their most important job will probably be reacquainting you with that strange and wonderful world outside your office walls.

HABIT: TARGET

You're already familiar with the information overload typical of a grant-seeking office. Because it's so easy to get distracted and waste time and resources, you target your work on getting exactly what you need and no more. When you interview program staff, you target certain staff people and ask questions that are most relevant to grant proposals. You target your work on your most grant-worthy programs, suggesting that your organization's other needs be covered by sources like individual giving or corporate sponsorships. In each grant request you target the match, asking for the program need that best matches the funder's interests.

As you gain experience seeking grants, your habit of targeting may lead you to focus on a few key working relationships that you've found particularly satisfying. You can connect directly with foundation staff, board members, and so on, on your own merits and out of your own interest. When you meet with them, you surprise them by asking about what they do, not what they can do for you. When it doesn't burden them, you can use them as resources for your current grant proposals and your own education as a grant seeker.

HABIT: LIMIT

You already know that as the number of people and pieces of paper involved in your grant requests climbs, your work becomes more complicated and wearisome. You limit your work to what's essential and become persuasive as well as productive. For instance, you limit your grant proposals to what funders need to know. You'll find they're easier to read that way. You limit the number of people involved in reviewing your proposals to those few staff who would be really responsible for using the money. You throw out all the documents you use except those you really need to keep.

As you learn systematic grant seeking, strict limiting is what allows you to take control of the process and get things done. But the point isn't to become a grant-seeking minimalist, with no friends and one-page grant proposals. Eventually the habit of limiting can evolve into one of balancing. You balance information going in and going out. You balance talking with program staff and watching their programs in action with the more technical business of prospect research and proposal assembly. You find an appropriate level of curiosity, friendship, and openness with funders. You balance the need to raise money with the need to go home and work in your garden.

HABIT: RESPECT

You are probably too familiar with the way a lot of people perceive the task of grant seeking: grants are manna from heaven or a version of noblesse oblige, obtainable by gambling, supplicating, or engaging in sly trickery. Although you're not naïve enough to think grants are always 100 percent fair, you've found it useful to approach grants as fair deals between colleagues. Your attitude is expressed by the respect you show the people you work with, inside and outside your organization.

You respect people's knowledge and positions, whether they're program officers from foundations or program directors from your organization. You meet with them when you have something to learn or communicate rather than for the sake of having face time. You respect the input you get from grant makers (as you would with any colleague), but you don't fawn over them or change your organization's programs just to make money. That would be disrespecting yourself.

As you become more experienced in grant seeking and spend less time and fuss on each proposal, you will have time to learn about the world of grant making beyond the contents of the latest grant guidelines. You can learn about the history of foundations and the issues they face from books like Dennis P. McIlnay's *How Foundations Work*[1] and the periodical *Foundation News & Commentary.*[2] You can learn the grant maker's point of view by reading draft proposals from other grant seekers or by serving on a committee that gives grants. For example, you might have one such committee at your local United Way. Giving away funds will certainly reinforce your respect for the grant maker's job. This respect will help you in your decision making about how to approach new prospects and long-time supporters when it's time for another proposal.

HABIT: CLEAR

You already know that grant seeking doesn't have to be the nightmare other people experience. You eliminate fuss like complicated databases and endless planning meetings and simply ask yourself, "What is the most direct path to funding?" Then whatever your answer is, you follow it. Maybe it's a recommendation that this project could be better funded by other kinds of fundraising; maybe it's a grant proposal to a carefully picked foundation. If it's the latter, you clear your writing, removing jargon and excessive detail that obscure the meaning of what your organization will do.

Even after you've been working as an efficient grant seeker for a while, it's possible to get bogged down in the average grant seeker's miasma of myths, fears, and inertia. You might find this reflected in your workspace, which can fill up with towers of file folders and unread copies of the local business journal. If this happens, clear away your newspapers and return to your organized *system*. Then clear away your fears and inertia by returning to your accomplishments and your values. Look at the infrastructure you've set up and the dozens of proposals that move in and out of your office. Think about the funding you've already won and the thousands of dollars (or more) that will come in the future, thanks to your investment. Think about the way that money will be used to make dreams come true and change lives. It may build a community center, take a child to the opera, educate a new home-owner, clean up a river, or plant a garden. When you need to, clear your mind of everything else and remember that you are making a difference. And you don't even need to stay up all night to do it.

NOTES

INTRODUCTION

1. Feczko, M. M., and Tobiasen, L. (eds.). *Foundation Directory, Part 2.* New York: The Foundation Center, 1995, p. vi.
2. Feczko and Tobiasen, p. vi.

CHAPTER ONE

1. McIlnay, D. P. *How Foundations Work: What Grantseekers Need to Know About the Many Faces of Foundations.* San Francisco: Jossey-Bass, 1998, p. 13.
2. Balzer, S. "Giving by Foundations Continues to Increase." *The Business Journal,* Phoenix, May 28, 1999, p. 7.
3. McPherson, S. *Oregon Foundation Data Book.* Portland, Ore.: C&D Publishing, 1999.

CHAPTER FOUR

1. PacifiCare Foundation. "Guidelines for Giving." [http://www.pacificare.com/corporate/about/foundation/guidelines.asp]. Feb. 2001.
2. Metropolitan Life Foundation. "Company Info: Community Involvement: MetLife Foundation." [http://www.metlife.com/Companyinfo/Community/Found/index.hml]. Feb. 2001.
3. Carpenter Foundation. "Annual Report, 1998–1999." Medford, Ore.: Carpenter Foundation, 1999.
4. David and Lucile Packard Foundation. "David and Lucile Packard Foundation." [http://www.packfound.org/]. Feb. 2001.

5. Avon Products Foundation, Inc. "Guidelines and Information." New York: Avon Products Foundation, Inc., 1998.

6. Ruddie Memorial Youth Foundation. "RMYF: About Us." [http://www.rmyf.org/aboutus/#jordan]. Sept. 2000.

7. H. B. Fuller Company Foundation. "H. B. Fuller: Community Affairs." [http://www.hbfuller.com/commenv/community/index.html]. Dec. 2000.

8. M. J. Murdock Charitable Trust. "Letter of Inquiry Instructions." [http://www.murdock-trust.org]. Feb. 2001.

9. M. J. Murdock.

10. A Territory Resource. "2001 Grant Application Kit." [http://www.atrfoundation.org/apply_for_a_grant.htm]. Feb. 2001.

11. U.S. Bank. "U.S. Bancorp/Community Relations." [http://www.usbank.com/comm_relations/cgform.html]. Feb. 2001.

12. GTE Foundation. "1998 Application Form." New York: GTE Foundation, 1998.

13. Douglas Community Foundation. "2000 Application Form." Roseburg, Ore.: Douglas Community Foundation, 2000.

14. W. K. Kellogg Foundation. "W. K. Kellogg Foundation." [http://www.wkkf.org]. Dec. 1999.

15. Avon, 1998.

16. GTE, 1998.

17. Murdock, 2001.

18. Whitney Houston Foundation for Children, Inc. "Format for Applying for Funds." [http://www.whfoundation.com/whfoundation/funds.html]. Feb. 2001.

19. Barbara Bush Foundation for Family Literacy. "National Grant Guidelines." [http://www.barbarabushfoundation.com/nga.html]. June 2000.

20. Murdock, 2001.

21. Murdock, 2001.

22. Kellogg, 1999.

23. Murdock, 2001.

24. Murdock, 2001.

25. Douglas, 2000.

26. H. B. Fuller, 2000.

27. Meyer Memorial Trust. "General Grant Guidelines." [http://www.mmt.org]. Jan. 2001.

28. Meyer, 2001.

29. Howard Wallis Irwin and Doris Carlyon Irwin Foundation. "Application Form." Portland, Ore.: Howard Wallis Irwin and Doris Carlyon Irwin Foundation, 2000.

30. Meyer, 2001.

CHAPTER SEVEN

1. Feczko, M. M., and Tobiasen, L. (eds.). *Foundation Directory,* Part 2. New York: The Foundation Center, 1995.

2. Zukowski, L. *Fistfuls of Dollars: Fact and Fantasy About Corporate Charitable Giving.* Redondo Beach, Calif.: EarthWrites, 1998, p. 41.

CHAPTER NINE

1. W. K. Kellogg Foundation. "W. K. Kellogg Foundation." [http://www.wkkf.org]. Dec. 1999.

2. Robinson, A. *Grassroots Grants: An Activist's Guide to Proposal Writing.* Berkeley, Calif.: Chardon Press, 1996.

CHAPTER TEN

1. Axelrod, T. "Asking for Money Naturally." *The Not-for-Profit CEO Monthly Letter,* Jan. 2001, *8,* p. 4.

CHAPTER SIXTEEN

1. McIlnay, D. P. *How Foundations Work: What Grantseekers Need to Know About the Many Faces of Foundations.* San Francisco: Jossey-Bass, 1998.

2. *Foundation News & Commentary.* Washington, D.C.: The Council on Foundations.

RESOURCE A:
HANDS-ON FORMS FOR GRANT SEEKERS

In this section you will find blank versions of all the forms referenced in the main text. Feel free to photocopy them. Use them in your meetings, research, and preparation for your own grant proposals.

Exhibit A.1. Questions About Our Organization

Mission and style

- When, why, and how did our organization start? Exactly who founded our organization?

- What is the story of our founding? Was it in response to a critical need or incident?

- What is the community need that we address? How is this need important to our community? Do we address the need on a local, regional, state, national, or global basis? What community or constituency do we serve or represent?

- What are our organization's values—the principles that drive our staff and board? How can we state our values positively? For instance, instead of saying "discrimination is wrong," might we say "we promote equality?"

- What does our organization want to achieve? What different ways can we express this, beyond our printed mission statement?

Direction

- How does our organization go about achieving our purpose? What are our major programs or projects? How do each of these programs contribute toward fulfilling our purpose?

- What are the top five accomplishments or milestones that best represent our history and growth? What are you most proud of that we've accomplished recently?

- Is there a timeline or written history of our organization?

- What about the future? Are we operating from a strategic plan, vision statement, or other overall plan? If so, how was it developed and by whom? May I have a copy of any written vision or plan?

Leadership

- Who is our board of directors? How would you describe them as a group? (For example, are they community leaders or experts in their fields?) Is there a printed list with affiliations, such as where board members work, and phone numbers?

- Is the board active? How often do they meet? How are board members selected? Is the board of an appropriate size? Is it growing, or is recruiting new and active board members currently a critical issue?

- How many nonboard volunteers do we have? Generally, what do they do? Do we know where they work, and is that information part of our database? If yes, whom do I ask for that information?

- How many paid employees do we have, and what do they do? What are the overall responsibilities of board, staff, and volunteers in comparison to one another?

- Are all segments of our constituency reflected in the power sharing and decision making of our organization? For example, if low-income single mothers are the constituency, how many low-income single mothers are on the board and in key volunteer or staff positions?

- Does our organization have a demonstrated commitment to diversity, such as a written policy statement, commitments in programs or work plans, public materials, or mission statement? If yes, may I have a copy of any written materials? If no, are we currently making an effort to develop a policy?

- Who are the key staff people for whom I should collect resumes or short bios?

Place in the community
- How does our organization respond to specific conditions that exist in our neighborhood, town, region, state, or country?
- Who else in our community does work similar to ours? How are we similar to these other groups, and how are we different? What makes our organization strategically valuable?
- How do we work together with other groups, formally or informally?
- Would you say our organization is a leader; if so, how? Are we the largest, first, or most knowledgeable in some area?

Resources
- What is our organization's total annual budget? Who are our top ten funding sources? Whom can I ask to run a list of these from our records?
- Are we a United Way agency?
- What is our breakdown of expenses? How much do we spend on administration? Programs? Other major categories appropriate to our organization?
- Whom do I ask for copies of individual budgets for each program and for the overall organization's financial statement?
- When was the most recent audit completed, and where do I get a copy?
- What nonfinancial resources do we have that are critical to our mission? For example, a specially designed or located building, an incredible volunteer base, a strong board of directors, or a crucial partnership with another organization?
- What is our current capacity to help our community? Are we able to serve, assist, inform, or include everyone who approaches us, or do we need to turn anyone away for lack of capacity or for any other reason? Are there people we'd like to be including but cannot reach out to? For what reason? What are our limits and limiting factors?

Impact in the community
- How would the world (or the city, county, state) be different *without* our organization? How would it be different in a concrete way and in an intangible way?

Exhibit A.2.   Questions About Our Program

Name and purpose
- What is the name of our program or project?
- What is the program's mission? How does it fit within our overall organization's mission and make sense given our values and other programs?

Community need
- Is this program new or ongoing?
- If this program is ongoing, why and when was it started? Is it expanding? If so, why?
- If the program is new, why is it being created? What is the specific community need for this program?
- Can you tell me the story of a person who needs this program?
- Do you know of any good sources for statistics to substantiate the need for this program? Would you give me copies of any reports or links to any Web sites you use?

Nuts and bolts
- If our program is new, is this a pilot phase? Of how long?
- If it is a one-time special project or event, what is its duration, including planning and post-event evaluation?
- If it is an ongoing program, what is the timeline for expansion?
- How does the program work? What are the specific services or goods the program will provide to the people it serves?
- How many people do we plan to serve or involve per year (or total, for one-time events)? What do these people have in common with one another?
- Are these people involved in the decision making and shaping of the program? If so, how?
- How long have you been planning this program?
- Do you have a specific work plan and timeline, and may I have copies of any printed plans?
- Is this program going to be produced solely by our organization or in partnership or collaboration with other organizations?
- If this is a collaboration, is the partnership formal, and do we have a letter of agreement? Or is it informal, in that our organizations rely on one another and enhance each other's work but don't have an official agreement?

Goals and vision
- What are our program's goals, objectives, and methods?
- What is your vision for the future of this program? If you had all the funding you desired, how would you operate the program? What's your dream in relation to this issue?

Resources

- What is the estimated cost for this project? If it is a multiple-year project, such as a three-year pilot phase or expansion phase, what is the total cost as well as each year's cost?

- May I have copies of any written budgets and any quotes from vendors or other documentation of how costs were arrived at?

- If the program is new, what specific things are needed to get it started?

- If the program is ongoing, what specific things are needed to keep going or to expand? Why seek a grant at this particular time?

- What resources are already in place for this project? Other grants or funding sources (and their amounts)? Donations? Physical resources, such as a space or vehicles? Volunteers?

- What other funding is being sought? Have proposals already been sent to any other potential funders? Are there reasons why particular funders might be interested?

- If the program is meant to continue in the future, how will it be funded after an initial grant or grants? Thinking creatively, how can we go beyond "looking for more grants"? For example, will the program cost less annually after it is established? Will it generate any of its own money through earned income? Is it especially appropriate for in-kind donations? Will it build philanthropy among a particular group of people who may give to it in the future?

- Who are the key personnel (paid or unpaid), and what are their qualifications? Do you have any written bios or resumes for them, or how can I reach them to ask about their qualifications? What portion of each person's time is going to be dedicated to this program or project?

Evaluation and impact

- How will our program be evaluated? Who will evaluate it and how often? What exactly will be measured to determine success?

- If the program is ongoing, has this evaluation been done before? What were the results?

- What will be done with future evaluation results? For example, will the program change as a result of evaluation feedback?

- In addition to the people who are directly served or involved, who else will our program affect? Think about this list of possible groups or people that the program will have an effect on:

direct participants?	health care providers?
their families?	faith centers or churches?
their children?	service clubs?
neighbors?	local businesses?
specific populations?	government?
schools?	other nonprofit organizations?
law enforcement?	other groups that are particular to our program or the whole community?

- Do you have letters of support from any of these groups, or could you identify two or three we can call to request letters?

Exhibit A.3. Considering a Match

Funder Name: _____

What size grants do they give (dollar range and average)? _____

How many grants did they make last year? _____

What percentage of these were given to organizations or programs similar to ours? _____

Among organizations or programs similar to ours, what was the average grant amount? _____

History
Grants they have made to our organization over the past five years: _____

_____

_____

Are there any notes in our files about conversations with foundation staff or trustees? If so, is there any indication of what the foundation would like to see next from us? _____

_____

Does anyone on our board know someone on theirs? _____

_____

Are there names of foundation staff I could call to ask for their guidance or ideas? _____

_____

Focus of grant making
Why did I think of this foundation in the first place? _____

_____

_____

What does the funder say they are interested in funding? _____

_____

Given my research, my impression about what this funder actually gives to is (try to go beyond project areas to trends; for example, does this funder seem to take risks on newer projects or organizations, or does this funder tend to give later in campaigns, after others have given?):

_____

_____

What project of ours comes to mind that seems to match best with their priorities? _____

_____

Does that project of ours have any specific grant-type needs at this time (remembering that grants are generally for new programs, expansions, capital purchases, and not ongoing, regular expenses)?

Item _____ estimated need $ _____

Item _____ estimated need $ _____

Item _____ estimated need $ _____

Item _____ estimated need $ _____

Item _____ estimated need $ _____

Do any of these estimated prices match or come closest to the average grants this foundation made to organizations similar to ours? Circle them, and concentrate on them first.

Think about whether these items seem to fit. For example, if they are capital, does this funder accept proposals for capital expenses?

Presentation

Why is it time to ask for a grant from this funder? Is the timing strategic for our organization? For the community? For this funder? _____

_____

Is our proposal an increase of some kind in our history with this funder? Is it enough to warrant a visit or tour? _____

_____

Will they schedule a meeting with us prior to sending a written proposal? _____

_____

Proposal Ideas or Next Steps

Exhibit A.4. Proposal Assembly Form

Use the first column of checkboxes to mark the pieces a particular funder requires or you want to attach. Then use the second column during proposal assembly to keep track of what you've actually attached.

Funder Name: _____

Requires _____ copies of proposal: Circle one: Bound or unbound?

Does each copy have to include attachments? _____

Does the narrative have to be on a form that they provide? _____

Whose signatures are required? Circle all that apply: program staff   CEO   board chair

Item	Required?	Attached
Cover sheet (their form or yours)	❏	❏
Organizational resume	❏	❏
Program resume	❏	❏
501(c)(3) letter from IRS	❏	❏
Board list (with or without board's affiliations)	❏	❏
Organizationwide budget	❏	❏
Organizationwide financial statement	❏	❏
Most recent audit	❏	❏
Previous audit	❏	❏
Program or project budget	❏	❏
Program or project financial statement	❏	❏
Most recent IRS Form 990	❏	❏
By-laws	❏	❏
Antidiscrimination policy or statement	❏	❏
Brochure or limited support materials	❏	❏
Letters of support (limit to truly relevant ones)	❏	❏
Other items you want to add (photos, artwork, etc.):	❏	❏
_____	❏	❏
_____	❏	❏
_____	❏	❏

Exhibit A.5. Fifteen Steps to a Proposal Narrative

1. What is our specific grant request (the amount and for what project)?

2. Who *is* our organization? What are its mission and brief history? Whom should the funder contact, and what is that person's phone number, mailing address, fax, and e-mail?

3. What is the community need that our organization, and specifically our project, addresses? What statistics and stories can we use to substantiate that need?

4. How does our proposed project address the need? What methods will we use? How many people will we serve or involve?

5. What are our measurable project goals or outcomes?

6. What is our timeline and work plan? Have we included everything from planning to evaluation?

7. Who are the key volunteers and staff on this project, and what are their qualifications? How much of their time will be spent on this particular project?

8. What is our projected cost and what are our sources of revenue? How will the project be sustained after the grant period, if applicable? (You can refer to an attached budget in this section.)

9. What other organizations in the community are providing similar programs or projects? How is ours different? How do we work together with the other providers?

10. Why is ours the right organization to launch this program, buy this item, or whatever it is we are proposing?

11. How will our program be evaluated, how often, and by whom? What will the evaluation process do for the program—will it help us adjust the program, replicate it in other cities, or plan in other ways?

12. Who and how many will benefit?

13. Why are we approaching this funder at this time?

14. How can we best thank the funder for their generosity and consideration?

15. What attachments will we be including?

Exhibit A.6. Project Summary Form

Use this form to prepare people in your organization for meetings or site visits with funders.

Name of funder: _____

Site visit on: _____ (date and time)

Or meeting on: _____ (date and time)

At: _____ (location)

Our staff or volunteers who will be attending: _____
_____

Funder representatives who will be attending: _____
_____

Purpose or main goal of meeting or visit: _____
_____

Funder's mission: _____
_____

A few typical grants they made last year:
_____
_____
_____
_____

Their grant range in dollars: _____

Name of our proposed project: _____

Grant amount we've requested:_____

One-sentence description of our project: _____
_____

Three key points about our project:

1. _____

2. _____

3. _____

Check one:

_____ We have already sent a proposal to this funder.

_____ We can have a proposal to this funder by _____ (date).

Exhibit A.7. Overall Tracking Form

Date of proposal	Funder name	Program or project proposed	Amount of request	Result	Result date

Exhibit A.8. Grant Follow-Up Form

Use this form to plan your follow-up activities once a grant has been received.

Funder name _____

Program funded _____

Person responsible for carrying out the funded program _____

    Phone _____ E-mail _____

Grant facts

Approximate grant dates	*Determination received*	*Check(s) received*	*Check(s) received*
Begin	Date	Date	Date
End	Amount	Amount	Amount

Restrictions on spending

_____

Follow-up action timeline

Under "required by," circle who is requiring this action—the funder or your organization—and write in the date it is due.

Required by	*Action*		*Completed*
Funder/Us	_____ _____	❏	_____ (date)
Funder/Us	_____ _____	❏	_____ (date)
Funder/Us	_____ _____	❏	_____ (date)
Funder/Us	_____ _____	❏	_____ (date)
Funder/Us	_____ _____	❏	_____ (date)
Funder/Us	_____ _____	❏	_____ (date)
Funder/Us	_____ _____	❏	_____ (date)

Final report due _____ form is theirs/ours

Final report mailed ❏ _____ (date)

Exhibit A.9. Staff Reminder Form

Date: _____

From _____

To: _____ (Program staff)

Re: Grant from _____ (funder)

    for $ _____ received on _____ (date),

    for _____ (program).

Please respond by _____ (date)

It's time to send a report or follow-up item to this funder.
Please send me any of the following you have available:

❏ Latest program statistics

❏ Most recent financial statement

❏ Any major changes to budget

❏ Any major changes to the project timeline

❏ Any changes to outcomes expected

❏ Any news of specific things you've been able to do with the grant money
   (equipment you've purchased, people you've hired, expanded hours)

❏ Photographs from the project or program, especially active ones

❏ Success stories of people who participated

❏ Letters of thanks from people who participated

❏ Any other items that would illustrate our progress

Thank you for helping me keep my files up to date and our funders informed.

Exhibit A.10. Grant-Seeking Ground Rules

As of _____ (date), the following policies and procedures apply to
grant seeking at _____ (organization).

*When filling out this form use titles rather than names, as staff may change in the future and you want
to keep a readable record.*

- The following personnel (staff or volunteers) will meet on a _____ (quarterly or
  semiannual or annual) basis to set priorities for grant seeking.

  _____

  _____

  _____

  _____

- This group will then communicate the priorities to the grant seeker or grant writer.
- This group will hold its first such meeting on _____ (date).
- The following personnel will be responsible for research on:

  Community needs and conditions _____

  _____

  Potential foundation funders _____

  _____

  Program needs (such as getting quotes from vendors)_____

  _____

  Other nonprofit organizations in our community _____

  _____

- _____ is responsible for giving the grants person timely updates on
  organizationwide budgets and financial statements.
- _____ is the first point of contact to foundation funders, and everyone should go through him or her to contact these funders.
- The following personnel have the authority to approve applying for grants at the following levels:

  _____ can approve ideas for grants up to $ _____

  _____ can approve ideas for grants up to $ _____

  _____ must approve ideas for all grants over $ _____

- Program directors (do/do not) have to approve all grant ideas that pertain to their programs.

- _____ is responsible for writing proposal narratives, with the
  following exceptions:

  _____

  _____

- The following personnel must be involved in proofreading grant proposal text before a proposal is mailed out. This list includes how much time these people need for review, how they wish to receive text for review, and whether they can be skipped over in the process if they are not available. (This portion of this form should be updated every time the involved personnel change.)

Title or position	Position is currently filled by	Ideal amount of time he or she needs to review grant text	Format he or she prefers for text to be reviewed (for example, e-mail attachment, hard copy)	Conditions under which this person can be eliminated from the approval process

- The following personnel are approved to sign grant applications:

  _____

  _____

  _____

  _____

- The grant seeker or grant writer (is/is not) approved to sign in the absence of these personnel (for example, if a deadline is approaching and the proper personnel are unavailable).

- The following are the situations when the board of directors will be involved in the grant-seeking process:

  _____

  _____

  _____

Exhibit A.10. Grant-Seeking Ground Rules, *continued*

- Only the following personnel should automatically receive copies of completed grant proposals:

  _____

  _____

  _____

- The following personnel need access to foundation files, and they will meet with the grant seeker to find out about them:

  _____

  _____

  _____

- _____ is responsible for sending official receipts, as required by the IRS, for foundation (and corporate?) grants.

- _____ is responsible for sending thank-you letters to foundation (and corporate?) donors.

- _____ is responsible for signing and returning grant agreements that may be required by funders, or is responsible for getting the proper signature from _____

- _____ is responsible for ensuring that all required follow-up and reporting is completed on time.

RESOURCE B:
COMPLETE SAMPLE GRANT PROPOSAL

TABLE OF CONTENTS

Cover Letter 222

The Thurston Family Foundation and
Port City Partnership for the Arts: Grant Narrative 223

Organizational Resume 228

Project Summary Sheet 229

2001 Board of Directors 230

Project Budget 231

Organizational Budget 232

Most Recent Audit 233

501(c)(3) Letter from the IRS 234

Letter of Support 235

Letter of Support 236

Cover Letter

Letterhead for Port City Partnership for the Arts
PO Box xxxx, Port City, CA xxxxx
Tel. 999.222.2222
www.webaddressforportcitypartnership.xxx

20 May 2001

Roz Foster
Program Director
The Thurston Family Foundation
PO Box xxxx
Port City, CA xxxxx

Dear Ms. Foster,

Wendy and I enjoyed meeting with you earlier this month. Thank you for taking the time to further explain the Thurston Family Foundation's history and goals, and to assist us with our funding request. The proposal you requested follows this letter.

At the Port City Partnership for the Arts, our mission for the past eight years has been to form strong connections and share expertise and audiences among the arts organizations of the Port City region. We facilitate scheduling of annual arts events and provide centralized membership, ticket sales, and fund development services to our members.

In our work, we and our members have perceived a growing need to interest and nurture audiences aged 20 to 40. "Project 21C" is designed to do just that, by engaging people new to arts attendance in a low-cost year-long program of education, events, performances, and social interaction.

I am writing to respectfully request a grant of $15,000 from the Thurston Family Foundation to establish Project 21C. Your donation will encourage 750 new arts-goers to learn about and enjoy the arts and will revitalize our city's cultural community for the new century.

I appreciate your consideration. Please call me or Oni Schuman, the Project Coordinator, with any questions or ideas.

Sincerely,

Jorge Klein
Executive Director

The Thurston Family Foundation and Port City Partnership for the Arts: Grant Narrative

Request

Port City Partnership for the Arts respectfully requests a grant of $15,000 from the Thurston Family Foundation to establish Project 21C, a year-round arts engagement program including education, performances/shows, and social gatherings. Project 21C provides access to the arts to people aged 20 to 40 who have typically not attended events and performances. The project builds the next generation of arts lovers and patrons in our region.

Port City Partnership for the Arts (PCPA)

As a Williams Art Foundation program officer, Mary Ryan heard repeatedly from applicants on two points: they needed to continually grow their audiences and reach out to new people, but they also needed to minimize their overhead expenses.

In 1990, Ryan left her post at the Williams Foundation to establish the Port City Partnership for the Arts to address these concerns. Most people said it couldn't be done, but Ryan and a core group of volunteers convinced the major arts organizations in Port City that by cooperating they could reach their goals more quickly and less expensively, and they could reach a larger and more diverse audience together than any of them could alone.

After two years of research and planning, the Partnership began full operations in 1992, with 12 member organizations. Today, PCPA has 32 members, which all recognize that they share a common pool of current and potential audiences and patrons. We facilitate shared annual scheduling of events and provide centralized and cost-effective marketing, public relations, fund development services, ticket sales, and evaluation surveys for all 32 members.

Community need

Though they have seen hours and hours of television, over a quarter of all Port City elementary school students have never seen a live play. Though many dream of being ballerinas, a full 90% of Port City kindergarten students have never been to the ballet. And according to Port City Public Schools, too many students report that they rarely or never paint or draw at home.

Yet Greg Sparks, Superintendent of Port City Public Schools, announced in his State of the Schools address this year that the arts open doors to other subjects, such as social studies, history, science, and math. He, like many others, recognizes the link between art appreciation, self-expression, and success in other areas of life.

Unfortunately, as our community's children grow older and graduate from high school and college, their interest in the arts often falls off entirely. In a recent survey, the Port City Arts Council found that only 32% of all adults ages 20 to 30 had attended either an opera, symphony, ballet, *or* theater performance in the past year. When questioned as to non-attendance, many cited feeling a barrier to attending, such as not knowing how to get tickets, not knowing where events are held, or not being able to afford tickets.

PCPA and our member organizations are concerned. This younger group, and those up to around age 40, are the future supporters and patrons of our arts organizations. As well, they are the parents of the following generation of arts lovers. The fact that they are perceiving strong barriers to participating in the arts may not only be limiting their own enrichment, but may also be devastating to the Port City cultural community's future.

We take this problem seriously and have formed a Leadership Team of volunteers who are community leaders *in this age group*. They requested we launch a project to actively seek out and engage new, young arts-goers. They have a vision for a city in which young individuals and families are *invited* to participate in the arts and to go beyond attendance to dialogue and understanding. "Project 21C" is the result of their vision.

Art Patrons for the 21st Century: "Project 21C"

Project 21C will develop the next generation of art supporters and patrons in Port City, by engaging young people new to arts attendance in a low-cost year-long program of arts education, events, performances, and social interaction. Project 21C will serve people will little experience attending our city's museums, galleries, ballet, symphony, theatre performances, and film festivals. It will be designed to encourage their enjoyment of and dialogue about the arts.

PCPA will maintain close communication with each new art-goer to keep them active and involved in the program for at least one year. Participants will be invited to be part of focus groups and surveys, which will return vital feedback to the region's arts organizations.

Measurable outcomes

Our goal is to create new interest in the arts among a young and vital segment of our population. We project that by the end of the first operating year:

- 750 first-time or infrequent arts-goers will have joined the program
- more than 400 will have attended at least six varied arts events or performances
- more than 400 will have received or participated in six or more related educational pieces
- at least 200 will have participated in three social gatherings to build on their enjoyment and promote dialogue on the arts.
- of 400 "graduates" from the program, at least 300 will show consistent, continued participation in arts events outside of the program in the 2 years following their participation.

Timeline

November 2001	Identify participants
	Continue planning with arts organizations
January 2002	First marketing mailing to potential participants
March 2002	Kickoff: First meeting of participants/workshop and social gathering
	Attendance at special opening of Museum's "Ten Years of Drek" show
May 2002	Educational Mailing for Port Rep's play "Trading Futures" by Jeanmarie Williams
	Mid-May, members attend performance to end Rep's season
July 2002	Gallery Night, social gathering and artists' presentation at 10 open galleries
August 2002	Educational mailing and participant survey
September 2002	Modern dance performance at Salamander
October 2002	"A Winters Tale" at Port Shakespeare Co.
	Actors and Directors talk following play

November 2002	"The Nutcracker" at The Ballet Company
	Project 21C Year 1 wrap-up party/social gathering for participants
	Identify group for Year 2
January-March 2002	Year 1 Participant Survey
	Marketing Mailing to Year 2 potential participants
Through 2003	Follow up with Year 1 participants and member organizations
	Year 2 activities, etc.

Key people

Project 21C was created and is driven by a 12-member volunteer Leadership Team, headed by Wendy Branch. Wendy is a 29-year-old mixed media sculptrix with an M.F.A. from Port University. Her work is shown locally at the Far Flung Gallery. Branch is also co-director of the Artists' Zoo, an innovative gallery and museum. Her community work includes volunteer fund raising for PCPA and for the Children's Organization, where she is currently Secretary of the Board. Her interest (as a spectator) in modern dance led her to get involved with building audiences for the local Salamander dance theatre, and fuels her interest in Project 21C.

Oni Schuman, Project 21C Coordinator, has a B.A. in Arts Administration from Port University, and has worked with PCPA for two years, first as an intern and then as Member Services Assistant. Oni's working relationships with member organizations, and her understanding of their needs, as well as her education, make her uniquely qualified to coordinate Project 21C. Oni will dedicate 100% of her time to this program.

Jorge Klein, PCPA Executive Director, has 18 years of experience in arts management. For 10 years, he was General Manager of Port Area Rep, where he instituted an incredibly successful subscription series program and the Sustainable Rep Endowment. More recently, Jorge acted as Interim Executive Director of the Port Shakespeare Company. He joined PCPA two years ago and has spent that time developing relationships with our member organizations and focusing on their needs, ideas, and dreams, as well as conducting community research into the current and potential audiences for the arts in Port City. He will give 25% of his time to Project 21C.

Financial resources

The first-year cost for Project 21C will be $275,000; a project budget is attached as per your request. A large portion of this budget is for subsidized tickets, to keep the project affordable for participants. Each participant will pay only $60 for a year's worth of educational mailings and programs, six performances and shows, and three additional gatherings. Therefore, we will rely on our most loyal funders, as well as new sponsors, to make this important program successful with people who are not accustomed to or not able to pay hundreds of dollars per year to participate in regional arts events. We already have $125,000 committed from the A Foundation and the B Foundation, and we have approached the Binkie Corporation for sponsorship, which is pending.

We are committed to the project long-term, so the 2000–01 budget includes $20,000 to carry us over into the beginning of Year 2 as well as funding for 25% of the salary of our Development Director, who will include this project in her annual fundraising strategy. We believe that this project will be especially attractive to some of our corporate sponsors, and we are creating a plan to approach them for Year 2 and beyond. This project is interesting in that it grows art patrons, many of whom may be in a position to support the project two or more years down the road. Therefore, graduates of the program will be added to our mailing list and targeted for giving to this project in the future.

Our place in the community

In Port City, PCPA is a unique organization. In fact, within our five-state region, we know of only one other non-governmental organization that brings together arts organizations in the way we do, providing centralized services and facilitating cooperation among entities who would typically be competing rather than working together.

Our nine years of experience in a field we essentially created makes us the one and only organization with the experience, mission, and existing partnerships to successfully carry out this program.

We work together with other providers, such as the Parks Department, Library, and University, as well as with our member organizations. Members that will participate in Project 21C include, but will not be limited to: Port City Art Museum, Far Flung Gallery, The Ballet Company, Port City Symphony, Port Area Rep, Salamander Theatre, Port Shakespeare Co., The Film Institute, Port University, and Port City Parks. Most of our partners have been involved in the planning of this program and are looking forward to providing arts events and educational materials to the project in its first two years. In return, they will build their audiences and receive important feedback from participants. The University and Parks Department will help us identify participants through their mailing lists of individuals who have signed up for or completed arts-related classes in the past two years, but who do not appear on any of the current subscriber or single-ticket-buyer lists at our arts organizations.

Success measurements

It is crucial that a new program make a real difference for *people,* and the PCPA has three levels of internal review that pertain to Project 21C and its impact on our member organizations and the participants.

1. *Quarterly Reports:* Quarterly reports will be completed by Oni Schuman, the Project Coordinator. These reports track the progress of Project 21C based on written standards that have been developed by our Leadership Team, and based on the measurable goals listed above in this proposal. Oni will work with participants to make sure the program is running in a way that makes them *want* to stay involved.

2. *Annual Member Review:* Each member organization has an opportunity and responsibility to participate in an in-depth, half-day-long review of PCPA once per year. This review process is led by Jorge Klein, Executive Director of PCPA, and takes a full month to complete with all 32 member organizations each year.

3. *Annual Performance Review:* Each staff member and volunteer of the PCPA receives an annual review to discuss their impact on PCPA programs over the past year and to set goals for the coming year. These reviews are carried out by each staff member's or volunteer's supervisor.

The benefits of Project 21C

A vital and active arts community is crucial to any healthy city. According to the Research in The Arts institute (RITA), participation in the arts increases self-esteem, problem-solving skills, and imagination at all ages, thereby benefiting our schools, universities, workplaces, families, and the entire community. RITA studies show that *active* participation in the arts (going beyond being a spectator and learning about/discussing art) increases these benefits three-fold and creates a positive ripple effect in families and workplaces where adults are more creative and confident.

People without prior arts experience or access must feel welcomed and engaged by our arts community in order to participate fully, so that we may all be more inspired by the work of our city's artists. The costs of losing our vital cultural community are too great to ignore. The benefits of Project 21C will include a more confident and creative workforce and community, and will also include a strong arts community for generations to come.

Project 21C and the Thurston Family Foundation

The Thurston Family Foundation has been, and continues to be, a crucial supporter of Port City's cultural community. We believe this project is a unique opportunity for you to invest in that cultural community for many years to come. Thank you for your focus on the arts, and thank you for your consideration of this request. A grant of $15,000 will bring the wonder and benefits of the arts to 750 more young people next year, and will create the positive ripple effects of a community actively engaged in the arts.

If you have any additional questions or suggestions, please call Jorge Klein or Oni Schuman at 999.222.2222, or see our web site at www.webaddressforportcitypartnership.xxx. We look forward to hearing from you.

Attachments

- Organizational "Resume"
- Project Summary Sheet
- Board list
- Project Budget
- Organizational Budget
- Most recent audit
- 501(c)(3) letter from the IRS
- Two letters of support

Port City Partnership for the Arts

PCPA was founded in 1992 to form strong connections and share expertise and audiences among the arts organizations of the Port City region. We are made up of 32 member arts organizations who recognize that they share a common pool of current and potential audiences and patrons. PCPA facilitates shared annual scheduling of events and provides centralized and cost-effective marketing, public relations, and fund development services, ticket sales, and evaluation surveys for our 32 member organizations.

History

1992   PCPA founded by Mary Ryan and 12 member arts organizations
1993   Published first annual arts calendar and combined member newsletter
1994   First opened for centralized ticket sales in downtown Port City
1998   Saved arts organizations $1 million in administrative costs since our founding—press conference & celebration
2000   Awarded the Community Partnership Award by the Mayor of Port City
2001   Recognized nationally as an Innovative Nonprofit Program by the Catalyst Institute

Current programs

- Marketing, development, and ticket sales for 32 member arts organizations
- Facilitate annual arts schedule for Port City region
- Develop audiences for the arts through educational programs
- Volunteer opportunities in every area of the arts and on our board and committees

Resources

Number of paid staff:	9
Number of volunteers:	57
Number of board members:	8
Board meets:	monthly
Total annual budget:	$1,156,500

Where our funding comes from:

Member arts organizations	28%
Foundation grants	39%
Corporate/business giving	18%
Special event revenue	9%
Individual donations	6%

Where it goes:

Staffing	41%
Member services	26%
Establishing Project 21C	24%
Printing	3%
Special event expenses	2%
Postage	1%
Insurance	1%
Transportation	1%
Communications	<1%

Contacts

Board President, Jeanmarie Williams, Tel. 999.333.2222
Executive Director, Jorge Klein, Tel. 999.222.2222
www.webaddressforportcitypartnership.xxx

Project Summary Sheet

Port City Partnership for the Arts
PCPA was founded in 1992, to help our member arts organizations reach broader audiences and build a sustainable, networked cultural community in Port City. We now have 32 member organizations, with a wide variety of missions and sizes.

Art Patrons for the 21st Century ("Project 21C")
Project 21C will develop the next generation of arts-goers and patrons in Port City, by engaging young people new to arts attendance in a low-cost year-long program of education, events, performances, and social interaction. Project 21C will serve people with little experience attending our city's museums, galleries, ballet, symphony, theatre performances, and film festivals.

Our goal is to create new interest in the arts among a young and vital segment of our population. We project that by the end of the first operating year:
- 750 first-time or infrequent arts-goers will have joined the program
- more than 400 will have attended at least six arts events and received 6 educational pieces
- long-term evaluation will show that participants have increased their arts attendance after the program period is over.

Our resources
- First-year cost: $275,000
- Already committed: $125,000 from the A Foundation and the B Foundation
- Volunteers: 12 local artists and young community leaders have formed a Leadership Team
- Each partner agency has agreed to assist PCPA in raising $10,000 toward the project.

Our partners
Port City Art Museum, Far Flung Gallery, The Ballet Company, Port City Symphony, Port Area Rep, Salamander Theatre, Port Shakespeare Co., The Film Institute, Port University, and Port City Parks

Our case
A vital and active arts community is crucial to any healthy city. Young people must feel welcomed and engaged by the arts in order to participate fully, so that we may all be better educated and more inspired by the work of our city's artists.

PCPA—a unique organization that brings together nonprofit arts entities who would typically be competing rather than working together—is the one and only organization with the experience, mission, and existing partnerships to successfully carry out this program.

Our contact information
Port City Partnership for the Arts Executive Director, Jorge Klein, 999.222.2222
Project 21C Coordinator, Oni Schuman, 999.222.2222
www.webaddressforportcitypartnership.xxx

2001 Board of Directors

Letterhead for Port City Partnership for the Arts
PO Box xxxx, Port City, CA xxxxx
Tel. 999.222.2222
www.webaddressforportcitypartnership.xxx

2001 Board of Directors

Board President:
Jeanmarie Williams
Director
Walleyed Productions
30 Columbia Place
Port City, CA xxxxx
Tel. 999.333.2222

Board Members:
Mary Ryan
Founder of PCPA
Former Director of the Williams Art Foundation
PO Box xxx
Port City, CA xxxxx
Tel. 999.333.2221

Lee Gregory
Attorney
250 XX Way
Port City, CA xxxxx
Tel. 999.333.2223

Mary Godinho
Owner & Curator
Far Flung Gallery
300 Hawthorne Way
Port City, CA xxxxx
Tel. 999.333.2224

Kevin Murphy
Vice President, Marketing
Binkie Corporation
1 Binkie Way
Port City, CA xxxxx
Tel. 999.333.2225

Christina Burke
Retired from Port City Public Schools
Also board member with The Ballet Company
2234 Tabbot Drive
Port City, CA xxxxx
Tel. 999.333.2226

Kimberly Kern
President & CEO
Drink Soda Enterprises
4545 Stark Drive
Port City, CA xxxxx
Tel. 999.333.2227

Dave Clark
Mixed Media Artist
55 Industrial
Port City, CA xxxxx
Tel. 999.333.2228

Project Budget

Port City Partnership for the Arts
Project 21C Annual Budget for 2001

REVENUES:

Thurston Family Foundation	$15,000	
Foundation A	100,000	
Foundation B	25,000	
Corporate Sponsorship	10,000	
Participants	45,000	*6 times 750 participants × $10*
Participating Member Arts Organizations	80,000	
TOTAL REVENUES		$275,000

EXPENSES

Project coordinator (including benefits)	$47,000	
25% of executive director's time (+ benefits)	22,500	
25% of development director's time (+ benefits)	13,500	
Subsidized arts tickets for 750 participants	67,500	*6 times 750 participants × $15*
Educational mailings	22,500	*6 times 750 participants × $5*
Post-event gatherings	30,000	*3 times 500 participants × $20*
Marketing	44,765	
Meeting expenses w/partner organizations	1,000	
Additional postage	1,200	
Phones	960	
Web site maintenance	2,500	
Transportation	1,575	
Carry over to year two	20,000	
TOTAL EXPENSES		$275,000

Organizational Budget

Port City Partnership for the Arts 2001 Budget

REVENUES:

Membership	$320,000	
Foundation grants	450,000	
Corporate and business giving	212,000	
Individual donations	74,500	
Special event revenue	100,000	
TOTAL REVENUES		$1,156,500

EXPENSES

Payroll and benefits	$473,000	
Establish Project 21C	275,000	
Marketing (our main service)	223,000	
Other member services	56,000	
Annual event	23,000	
Database management and equipment	23,000	
Printing	32,000	
Postage	14,000	
Newsletters	8,000	
Phones	4,200	
Internet	660	
Insurance	12,000	
Transportation	12,000	
TOTAL EXPENSES		$1,155,860

Most Recent Audit

(Note: The audit will be multiple pages; we show only the cover sheet here.)

Independent Audit of Port City Partnership for the Arts
by
Bruce & Bruce
Port City, CA xxxxx
May 26, 2000

501(c)(3) Letter from the IRS

INTERNAL REVENUE SERVICE
DEPARTMENT OF THE TREASURY
ADDRESS
ADDRESS

Port City Partnership for the Arts
199 Market Street Suite 1300
Port City, CA xxxxx

Employer Identification Number:
    9x-xxxxxxx
Case Number:
    XXXXXXXXX
Contact Person:
    E. GAMBLE
Contact Telephone Number:
    213.XXX.XXXX
Our Letter Dated:
    August 26, 1993
Addendum Applies:
    No

Dear Applicant:

This modifies our letter of the above date in which we stated that you would be treated as an organization that is not a private foundation until the expiration of your advance ruling period.

Your exempt status under section 501(a) of the Internal Revenue Code as an organization described in section 501(c)(3) is still in effect. Based on the information you submitted, we have determined that you are not a private foundation within the meaning of section 509(a) of the Code because you are an organization of the type described in section 509(a)(1) and 170(b)(1)(A)(vi).

Grantors and contributors may rely on this determination unless the Internal Revenue Service publishes notice to the contrary. However, if you lose your section 509(a)(1) status, a grantor or contributor may not rely on this determination if he or she was in part responsible for, or was aware of, the act or failure to act, or the substantial material change on the part of the organization that resulted in your loss of such status, or if he or she acquired knowledge that the IRS had given notice that you would no longer be classified as a section 509(a)(1) organization.

If we have indicated in the heading of this letter that an addendum applies, the addendum enclosed is an integral part of this letter.

Because this letter could help resolve any questions about your private foundations status, please keep it in your permanent records.

Sincerely yours,

THE IRS! SAMPLE LETTER ONLY!

Letter of Support

Wendy Branch
The Artists' Zoo
25 Industrial
Port City, CA xxxxx

18 May 2001

Jorge Klein
PCPA
PO Box xxxx
Port City, CA xxxxx

Dear Jorge,

I am writing to support PCPA's application to fund Project 21C—a project which is dear to me and to the volunteer Leadership Team of which I am the Chairperson.

When the Leadership Team first met, we knew we were charged with studying and finding solutions for the lack of younger arts audiences. In our research process, we have been supported by Oni Schuman and the other staff at PCPA, but have been responsible for driving our own project and creating our own vision.

I would like our potential funders to know that Project 21C will continue to be driven by this Leadership Team, made up of 12 volunteers who are all under the age of 40 and are involved in the local arts scene, from visual arts to theater and ballet. We are excited that our vision is being supported so entirely by PCPA, and that we will have the opportunity to make an incredible difference for the future of our city.

Thank you,

Wendy Branch
Co-Director, The Artists' Zoo
Volunteer, PCPA

Letter of Support

Port City Art Museum
22 Main Street
Port City, CA xxxxx

10 May 2001

Jorge Klein
PCPA
PO Box xxxx
Port City, CA xxxxx

Dear Jorge,

It's my pleasure to write in support of Port City Partnership for the Arts and the new Project 21C. The Port City Art Museum was proud to be among the first organizations to join and help form PCPA in the 1990s. Since that time, the amount of administrative expenses and time that we have saved—and been able to dedicate to art instead of fund raising—has been incredible. PCPA's support of our membership services has meant more time for us to work with individual major donors, and has resulted in more and better museum services for our community. PCPA is a lifesaver for our organization.

Over the past decade, the Museum has become increasingly concerned about the changing demographics of Port City and our attendees. We are very pleased that PCPA is taking an initiative to involve more young people and families in our cultural community.

This is an important project, for which the Museum has committed to raising at least $10,000 from our own donor pool, separate from PCPA. We believe this is a small price to pay for the opportunity to build future support and interest in our cultural heritage. We look forward to working together further on the planning and implementation of Project 21C.

Sincerely,

Carl Sorensen
Director
Port City Art Museum

INDEX

A

Academics, 73. *See also* Community need
Acceptance, 156–157. *See also* Funding decisions
Acrobat Reader, 26, 85
Adobe, 26, 85
American Association of Fund Raising Counsel, 11
Answer paragraphs, 122
Anticipating, as work habit, 197
Antidiscrimination policy, 28, 61
Aspen Publishers, 84
Association of Fundraising Professionals, 84
Axelrod, T., 136

B

Base materials: appearance of, 60–62; gathering, 59–60; and organizational and program resumes, 62–68
Bill and Melinda Gates Foundation, 15, 190
Biographies. *See* Bios
Bios, 27, 61
Black United Fund of Oregon, 139
Board members list, 27, 61

Board-to-board relationships, 137–138. *See also* Business relationships
Branch, W., 124
Brown, A., 142
Business journal, 199
Business relationships: and board-to-board relationships and communications, 137–138; establishing, 135–136; and staff-to-staff relationships, 138–139
Bylaws, 28, 60

C

Carnegie Foundation, 13
Case statement, 35
Charities Registrar, 81, 99
Chronicle of Philanthropy, 85
Clearing, as work habit, 199–200
Community files, 29
Community need: and academics, 73; and government agencies, 72; and Internet, 71; and librarians, 73; and newspapers, 72; quantification of, 69–71; stories about, 74–75
Corporate Grants Alert, 84
Council on Foundations, 85
Cover letter, 127–128

Cubist grants, 126
Cycles, 196–197

D
Deadline cards, 91, 119, 160, 167
Deadline file, 160, 165, 166
Deadline tracking system, 26–27

E
Evaluation: and assessment of opportunities, 165–167; and celebration of success, 172; of financial goals, 169–170; and first-priority program, 55–57; and goal setting, 167–172; and grant-seeking cycle, 19; and making ground rules, 190–192; of nonfinancial goals, 170–171; and one-year review, 171–172; of success rate, 168–169

F
FedEx, 3, 7
Files: community, 27, 29; funder, 27, 29–30; organization and program, 27–28; paper *versus* computer, 28–29; special, 30–31
Filing, 27–31, 89–90
Financial statements, 27
Fistfuls of Dollars (Zukowski), 91
Folders, making, 92
Follow-up: expediting process of, 160–161; in grant-seeking cycle, 18; and making ground rules, 187–189; need for honesty in, 161–162; plan for funding decisions, 157–160; three kinds of, 158. *See also* Funding decisions
Folsom, J. T., 139
Foundation Center, 78, 79, 80, 84
Foundation Data Books, 81

Foundation Directory (Feczko and Tobiasen), 79, 80
Foundation Grants Index (Foundation Center), 79, 80
Foundation News & Commentary, 82, 199
Funder files, 27, 29–30
Funding decisions: and acceptance, 156–157; driving follow-up process to, 160–161; follow-up plan for, 157–160; need for honesty in follow-up to, 161–162; and rejection, 155–156; three kinds of follow-up to, 158

G
Goals: financial, 169–170; and first-priority program, 51–53; nonfinancial, 170–171; setting, 167–172
Government agencies, 72. *See also* Community need
Grant Follow-Up Form, *159*
Grant seeking: fear of, 3–4; ground rules for, 179–192; misconceptions about, 4–15; spray and pray method of, 5
Grants: consistent usefulness of, 11–13; and importance of pinpointing matches and tailoring proposals, 9; and "knowing somebody," 9–11; as most frequently small, numerous, and local, 13–14; myths about, 4–15; and program control, 14–15; as rational deals between colleagues, 4–7; writing proposals for, as predictable and simple, 7–8
Grant-seeking cycle, *18*; and evaluation, 19; and follow-up, 18; and invitation, 18; and learning, 17; and matching, 17–18; operation of, 19–20; personalization of, 173–178; timing in, 20–21; understanding, 17–19
GrantSmart.org, 99

Grassroots Grants (Robinson), 131

Ground rules: and definition of responsibilities and roles, 182–183; and evaluation, 190–192; and follow up, 187–189; initial summit for, 180–183; and inviting, 185–187; and learning, 183–184; and matching, 185; second summit for, 183–192; setting priorities for, 180–182; writing-up, 192

Guidestar.org, 99

H

How Foundations Work (McIlnay), 4, 199

I

Information overload, 88–90

Inquiries, making, 86–88

Internal Revenue Service (IRS), 27, 59, 62; 501(c)(3) letter, 27, 59–60, 119, 120; Form 990-PF, 27, 59–60, 99

Internet: and community need, 71; and generating leads, 85–86

Interview, personal, 36

Introductory call, 115–117

Invitation: assembling proposal or letter of inquiry for, 117–128; deciding on initial approach for, 111–112; editing proposal for, 128–132; in grant-seeking cycle, 18; and making ground rules, 185–187; and making introductory call, 115–117; and meetings with funders, 139–142; and tour or site visit, 115–117

K

Key people, bios of, 61. *See also* Bios

Krohn, P., 36

L

Leadership, organizational, 40–42

Leads, generating: and definition of lead, 77–78; and Foundation Center Libraries and cooperating collections, 78; and *Foundation Directory,* 79–80; and information overload, 88–90; and Internet, 85–86; and the library, 78; and locally published guides, 81; and making inquiries, 86–88; and newspapers and trade periodicals, 81–82; and other fundraisers, 83–84; paid search services for, 86; and periodicals, 84–85; and periodicals about philanthropy, 82–83; and screening of potential funders, 90–92; volunteers, 83

Learning: in grant-seeking cycle, 17; and making ground rules, 183–184

Letter of inquiry (LOI), 118–119

Library, 73, 78. *See also* Community need

Limiting, as work habit, 198

M

Match: angle of approach for, 103–105; current grant-making focus of, 102–103; definition of, 97–98; giving pattern of, 99–100; in grant-seeking cycle, 17–18; past history with, 100–102; and timing of proposal, 105–107

Matching: in grant-seeking cycle, 17–18; and making ground rules, 185

McIlnay, D. P., 4, 199

McMahon, E., 9

Meeting, with funders, 139–142

Microsoft, 190; Excel, 121

Mission, 37–39

Mission creep, 8

N

Narrative, proposal: free-form, 121–126; funder-structured, 126–127

Newspapers: clippings, 28; and community need, 72; and generating leads, 81–82

Nonprofit World Funding Alert, 84

O

Office space: and community files, 29; and deadline tracking system, 26–27; essential files for, 27–31; and funder files, 29–30; and information processing system, 23–24; materials for, 24–26; need for, 23–24; and organization files, 27–28; and paper *versus* computer files, 28–29; resources for, 25–26; space for, 24–26; and special files, 30–31

Opportunities, assessment of, 165–167

Oregon, 13, 62

Oregon Children's Foundation, 142

Oregon Foundation Data Book (McPherson), 13

Organization: budget for current year, 27; case statement for, 35; direction of, 39–40; files, 27–28; impact of, in community, 45; leadership in, 40–42; mission of, 37–39; and personal interview, 36; place of, in community, 42–43; story of, 36; style of, 37–39; use of resources by, 43–45

Organizational resume, 27, 62–68, *64–65*

Orlo Foundation, 36, 39

Overall Tracking Form, *149*, 153, 155, 157

P

Pacific Northwest, 23

Paid search services, 86

Periodicals: about philanthropy, 82–83; and generating leads, 84–85; trade, 81–82

Personalization, 173–178

Pew Charitable Trust, 13, 14

Philanthropy, periodicals about, 82–83

Port City Partnership for the Arts, 123

Portland, Oregon, 36, 62, 143, 190

Program, first-priority: basic facts about, 49–51; evaluation of, 55–57; goals and visions of, 51–53; identifying, 46–47; impact of, 55–57; name and purpose of, 47–48; need addressed by, 48–49; resources for, 53–55

Program resumes, 62–68, *66*

Project budget, sample of, *122*

Project Summary Form, 140, *141*, 143

Proposal: argument clarity and style of, 131; assembling, 117–128; attachments for, 119–120; budget for, 120–121; colleagues' review of, 128–130; cover sheet and cover letter for, 127–128; editing, 128–132; free-form narrative for, 121–126; funder-structured narrative for, 126–127; general presentation of, 130–131; letters of inquiry (LOI) *versus* full, 118–119; need for, 117; and outside readers, 131; parts of, 119–128; and sample project budget, *122*; second draft of, 132

Proposals, follow-up: and communication with development coworkers, 153–154; and communication with own board of directors, 152–153; and communication with own organization's staff, 151–152; and communication with prospective funder, 150–151; finishing with, 147–149; tracking of, 149–150

Prospect: and communication with prospective funder, 150–151; definition of, 98

R

Rejection, 155–156
Research in The Arts (RITA) institute, 125
Respect, as work habit, 198–199
Review, one-year, 171–172
RFP Bulletin (Foundation Center), 84
Robinson, A., 131
Rockefeller Foundation, 13
Ryan, M., 123

S

Salvation Army, 23, 143, 190
Screening, 90–92
Search services, paid, 86
Site visit, 115–117, 142–144
SMART (Start Making A Reader Today) literacy program, 142
Society for Nonprofit Organizations, 84
Staff-to-staff relationships, 138–139. *See also* Business relationships
Stories, 27, 36, 74–75. *See also* Community need
Success: celebration of, 165–167, 172; rate of, 168–169

T

Targeting, as work habit, 197–198
Tax returns, 99
Thurston Family Foundation, 123, 125
Timing, 20–21, 105–107
Tour, 115–117, 142–144

U

United States Department of Justice, 81
United Way, 44, 81, 90, 199

V

Volunteers, 83

W

Williams Art Foundation, 123
Work habits: and anticipating, 197; and clearing, 199–200; and limiting, 198; and respect, 198–199; and targeting, 197–198

Z

Zukowski, L., 91